CLOCKS

Chronicling Time

These and other books are included in the
Encyclopedia of Discovery and Invention
series:

CLOCKS
Chronicling Time

by A. J. Brackin

The ENCYCLOPEDIA of
D·I·S·C·O·V·E·R·Y
and INVENTION

P.O. Box 289011 SAN DIEGO, CA 92198-0011

For Merci, who brightened my past,
and Amy, who brightens my future.

The editor wishes to thank Carol Sowell for her
contribution to this book.

Library of Congress Cataloging-in-Publication Data

Brackin, A. J., 1958-
   Clocks: chronicling time / by A. J. Brackin.

   p. cm.—(The Encyclopedia of discovery and invention)
   Includes bibliographical references and index.
   Summary: Examines early concepts of time; describes
devices for measuring time and the improvements in their
technology: and discusses how measured time has shaped
our concepts of work and leisure.
   ISBN 1-56006-208-8
   1. Clocks and watches—Juvenile literature.   2. Time—
Juvenile literature [1. Clocks and watches.   2. Time]
I. Title.   II. Series.
TS542.5.B68 1991
681.1'13—dc20   91-16713

Contents

■ ■

Foreword

The belief in progress has been one of the dominant forces in Western Civilization from the Scientific Revolution of the seventeenth century to the present. Embodied in the idea of progress is the conviction that each generation will be better off than the one that preceded it. Eventually, all peoples will benefit from and share in this better world. R.R. Palmer, in his *History of the Modern World*, calls this belief in progress "a kind of nonreligious faith that the conditions of human life" will continually improve as time goes on.

For over a thousand years prior to the seventeenth century, science had progressed little. Inquiry was largely discouraged, and experimentation, almost nonexistent. As a result, science became regressive and discovery was ignored. Benjamin Farrington, a historian of science, characterized it this way: "Science had failed to become a real force in the life of society. Instead there had arisen a conception of science as a cycle of liberal studies for a privileged minority. Science ceased to be a means of transforming the conditions of life." In short, had this intellectual climate continued, humanity's future would have been little more than a clone of its past.

Fortunately, these circumstances were not destined to last. By the seventeenth and eighteenth centuries, Western society was undergoing radical and favorable changes. And the changes that occurred gave rise to the notion that progress was a real force urging civilization forward. Surpluses of consumer goods were replacing substandard living conditions in most of Western Europe. Rigid class systems were giving way to social mobility. In nations like France and the United States, the lofty principles of democracy and popular sovereignty were being painted in broad, gilded strokes over the fading canvasses of monarchy and despotism.

But more significant than these social, economic, and political changes, the new age witnessed a rebirth of science. Centuries of scientific stagnation began crumbling before a spirit of scientific inquiry that spawned undreamed of technological advances. And it was the discoveries and inventions of scores of men and women that fueled these new technologies, dramatically increasing the ability of humankind to control nature—and, many believed, eventually to guide it.

It is a truism of science and technology that the results derived from observation and experimentation are not finalities. They are part of a process. Each discovery is but one piece in a continuum bridging past and present and heralding an extraordinary future. The heroic age of the Scientific Revolution was simply a start. It laid a foundation upon which succeeding generations of imaginative thinkers could build. It kindled the belief that progress is possible as long as there were gifted men and women who would respond to society's needs. When Antonie van Leeuwenhoek observed *Animalcules* (little animals) through his high-powered microscope in 1683, the discovery did not end there. Others followed who would call these "little animals" bacteria and, in time, recognize their role in the process of health and disease. Robert Koch, a German bacteriologist and winner of the Nobel Prize in Physiology and Medicine, was one of these men. Koch firmly established that bacteria are responsible for causing infectious diseases. He identified, among others, the causative organisms of anthrax and tuberculosis. Alexander Fleming, another Nobel Laureate, progressed still further in the quest to understand and control bacteria. In 1928, Fleming discovered penicillin, the antibiotic wonder drug. Penicillin, and the generations of antibiotics that succeeded it, have done more to prevent premature death than any other discovery in the history of humankind. And as civilization hastens toward the twenty-first century, most agree that the conquest of van Leeuwenhoek's "little animals" will continue.

The *Encyclopedia of Discovery and Invention* examines those discoveries and inventions that have had a sweeping impact on life and thought in the modern world. Each book explores the ideas that led to the invention or discovery, and, more importantly, how the world changed and continues to change because of it. The series also highlights the people behind the achievements—the unique men and women whose singular genius and rich imagination have altered the lives of everyone. Enhanced by photographs and clearly explained technical drawings, these books are comprehensive examinations of the building blocks of human progress.

CLOCKS

Chronicling Time

CLOCKS

Introduction

What time is it? No matter where you are, this simple question can probably be answered quickly, easily, and accurately. In industrialized societies, time is of the utmost importance: jobs, appointments, school, lessons, and countless other activities start and end at proscribed times. Our dependence on clocks is so complete and automatic that we rarely question the universality and reliability of these machines that tick out the minutes of our daily lives. But there are societies that have no such dependence, even today. For the story of the clock is inextricably tied to the development of industry.

Not so long ago, in fact, even most Americans had little need for clocks. The farmers, settlers, and craftspeople who lived in early America used the sun to dictate their long days—they got up and started work at dawn, and they finished work when the sun set. Today, some rural societies still live this way. There is simply nothing in these rural cultures that requires the precise counting of the hours. In fact, the first mechanical clocks, ironically, were playthings for the wealthy—people who had the least reason to keep track of their days. These clocks were ornate, beauti-

■■■ TIMELINE: CLOCKS

1 > 2 >3 > 4 > 5 > 6 > 7 > 8 >

1 ■ 3000 B.C.
The Sumerians divide each day into twelve parts.

2 ■ 1500 B.C.
The Egyptians use sundials to keep track of the passage of time.

3 ■ 1400 B.C.
The Egyptians build water clocks.

4 ■ A.D. 1000
Clock escapement is invented.

5 ■ 1300
The foliot balance is first used to further refine the escapement.

6 ■ 1321
Tower clocks using the escapement and foliot balance become popular, especially in England.

7 ■ 1504
German locksmith Peter Henlein builds the first watch.

8 ■ 1577
One of the first minute hands is added to a clock.

9 ■ 1656
Christian Huygens first uses a pendulum in a clock.

10 ■ 1760
English carpenter John Harrison completes his fourth and most successful marine chronometer.

ful, and completely inaccurate.

In the cities, however, timekeeping gained importance. Employers needed to keep track of the number of hours people worked—and how much to dock them if they arrived late or left early. Children attending school or working alongside their parents in the factories were also expected to arrive on time. Buses, railroads, and trolleys ran on time schedules. It is interesting to note that railroad stations and employees were thought to have the most accurate timepieces, the better to schedule the arrivals and departures of the trains. It did not take long for clocks to begin to dominate people's days.

Clocks perform other functions, besides the most obvious mentioned here. There are clocks that the average person knows little about, but are a necessity to science. Clocks drive satellites, telescopes, and scientific experiments designed for studying nature's laws. They allow precise calculations that could never have been made before their invention and development.

The invention of the clock is a fascinating tale that is inextricably woven with the development of human civilization. *Clocks* recounts the history of these objects that are such a permanent part of our existence.

11 ■ 1803
Eli Terry uses machines to mass-produce pieces for thousands of inexpensive clocks.

12 ■ 1884
Twenty-six countries agree that Greenwich, England, will serve as a common starting point for worldwide time zones and determining longitude.

13 ■ 1914
Wristwatches become popular in the United States; American inventor Henry Warren designs the first electric clock.

14 ■ 1948
The first atomic clock is developed by physicist Louis Essen in England.

15 ■ 1949
Timex, the first inexpensive wristwatch, is marketed.

16 ■ 1960
Accutron, the first electronic wristwatch, is created.

17 ■ 1967
The first atomic clock using cesium is developed.

18 ■ 1989
Atomic clocks are improved to keep time accurately to within one second every three million years.

CHAPTER 1

Nature's Clocks

No one is sure how long ago people started keeping track of time. But when they did, people did not use clocks that precisely told them the hours, minutes, and seconds in a day. Those kinds of clocks were invented only about seven hundred years ago.

Before then, people probably got a sense of time from the rhythm of the day and the change of seasons throughout the year. They were aware that night followed day, then day came again, and then the cycle repeated. Someone somewhere probably noticed that shadows cast by trees grew longer as the day passed and that the sun moved farther west in the sky. Eventually, people probably used the length of a shadow to determine times for meetings. They would agree to meet when the shadow of a certain tree was as long as a person's foot or when the shadow reached a rock. The ancient Sumerians, who lived more than five thousand years ago in the area where Iraq is located today, are believed to have been the first people to try measuring the passing day by using shadows.

The Sumerians built a civilization that included religion, government, and literature. They also had a calendar with seven-day weeks, with each day divided into twelve equal parts. Each of these twelve parts lasted about two of our hours today. However, the exact length of these Sumerian hours varied with the seasons. Sumerian hours were shorter during the winter when there

The ancient Egyptians used this huge, needle-shaped sundial to tell time. One of a pair originally erected in Egypt in the fifteenth century B.C., it now stands in New York City's Central Park.

The sun shines on a garden sundial built in 1718. The piece that casts the shadow is called a gnomon.

was less sunlight and longer in the summer when there was more sunlight.

By dividing the day into twelve parts, the Sumerians were able to keep track of the passage of time. But they could not pinpoint specific times of day. Little evidence has been found to explain exactly how the Sumerians kept track of time or why they wanted to do so. Historians believe it probably had something to do with their religious observances.

When the Sumerian people were conquered around 2370 B.C., nearly all traces of their timekeeping techniques disappeared with them. Historians say more than six hundred years passed before other civilizations made similar efforts to keep track of time. These efforts would be among the first of many.

Sundials

Like the Sumerians before them, the ancient Egyptians divided the day into twelve time periods. They kept track of

these time periods with huge granite columns that thinned at the top into a point. These columns are called "Cleopatra's needles," named for the queen who ruled Egypt from 51 to 30 B.C. On the ground around the columns were twelve marks for the twelve divisions of the day. When the sun touched the top of the needle, a shadow fell on the ground. The length and position of the shadow told the Egyptians how much daylight remained. As the sun moved across the sky, the shadow cast onto the marks grew longer. Early in the morning, the shadow touched only the first one or two lines. By afternoon, shadows covered most of the marks, and by sunset, all twelve were in shadows.

The Egyptians came to rely on the needles for keeping track of the passage of time. But the height of one needle—nearly seventy feet tall—and its weight—about 220 tons—made it an impractical timekeeping piece for the average person. So the Egyptians developed a smaller, portable timekeeping

SUNDIALS

GNOMON

Sundials tell time by measuring the sun's daily path across the sky. Although there are many different types of sundials, most consist of a pointer, called a style or gnomon, and a plate on which the gnomon casts a shadow. The position and length of the shadow cast by the gnomon on the dial changes as the sun moves across the sky and, in this way, indicates the time of day. At midday, when the sun is directly overhead, for example, the gnomon casts a shadow over the 12 o'clock line.

piece called a sundial. The sundial worked like the larger needles and had three parts: a circular dial marked with lines but no numbers; a needlelike object in the middle of the dial; and a triangular or rectangular piece of wood or metal, called a style, for holding the needle upright. When the sun touched the needle, it cast a shadow on the lines marked on the dial, showing how much daylight had passed and how much remained. Although all sundials had these three basic parts and worked in the same way, the Egyptians invented many different designs. On some, the dial was a flat circle, while other dials were rounded like bowls or straight and bar-shaped.

Like the Egyptians, the early Romans also kept track of the passing day. Initially, they did so without the help of sundials. During this period, the Romans divided the day into only two parts: day and night. They depended on public criers to announce the rising and setting of the sun, according to the

Sundials came in many shapes and sizes. This pocket sundial from China measures six inches by four inches.

writings of a first-century Roman historian named Pliny. It was only after they defeated the Egyptians in war around 30 B.C. that the Romans learned about sundials. Among the many prizes the Romans took home with them from Egypt was one of Cleopatra's needles. The Romans called their prize a gnomon, which means "one who knows." This name is still used for the needle that stands in the middle of a sundial.

Despite their efforts to adapt the Egyptian sundials to their own purposes, the Romans were unable to do so. The Roman sundials frequently showed different shadow lengths at the same times on different days. At noon, for example, the shadow cast by the gnomon might be two inches long one day and three inches long the next. Or the shadow might be straight out to the right one day and straight up another day.

It would be several centuries before an Iranian astronomer named Al-Battani would figure out what the Egyptians knew and the Romans never discovered: no sundial will accurately keep time unless the needle is positioned correctly. In the ninth century, Al-Battani found that in order for the shadow cast by the gnomon to be the same length at the same time each day, the gnomon always had to point toward the North Star. He also wrote that the proper angle and height of the gnomon varied with the distance of the sundial from the equator. The farther from the equator, the higher the gnomon needed to be for the sundial to work accurately.

Despite the problems the Romans had, the Egyptian sundials were quite good at keeping time. Yet these time-keeping pieces did have some limitations. Most important, they did not work at all when it was cloudy or raining or at night. These disadvantages probably inspired ideas for other timekeeping devices.

Water Clocks

The Egyptians used water as well as sun for measuring time. The simplest and earliest of their water clocks consisted of a small bucket of water with a tiny hole in the bottom. They measured the passage of time by the flow of water from the bucket. Larger buckets were used to keep track of longer time periods. Like sundials, water clocks showed the passage of time but did not keep track of the exact hours in a day.

Although the early Egyptians were probably the first to build water clocks, theirs were not the most advanced. The Greek water clock, called a clepsydra,

Later water clocks were more elaborate. Some had several bowls and buckets attached. When the water ran out of one bowl, it filled another. As that one ran out, it emptied into a third bowl. Some of these clocks even had bowls with little wooden ducks floating on the water. A rope was tied to each duck. As the water level dropped, and the duck sank lower, the rope pulled a hand around a nearby dial. The dial was marked with numbers, and the hand pointed to a number that showed how much time had passed.

Around 250 B.C., the Greek mathematician and inventor Archimedes is said to have built an even more elaborate water clock. This clock apparently

The Greek mathematician and inventor Archimedes is said to have built an elaborate water clock around 250 B.C.

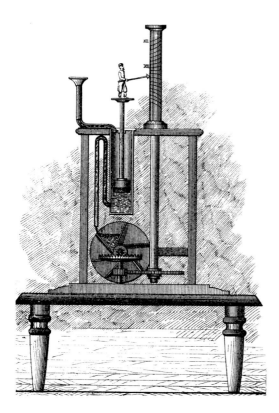

This diagram depicts a clepsydra, or water clock, thought to have been created in the second century B.C. by a Greek inventor named Ctesibius of Alexandria.

which means "water thief" in Greek, was often a complex instrument. A typical clepsydra consisted of a bowl with a small hole placed inside a large bucket of water. When the bowl filled with water, it sank, indicating that a certain amount of time had passed.

In both Greece and Rome, water clocks were used to measure how long lawyers spoke in court. When the bowl sank, the speaker's time was up. Usually, an officer of the court was responsible for making sure that the water in the bucket stayed at a constant level. The court officer also had to watch for pebbles or gravel that might clog the bowl's opening, slowing the water's flow and increasing the time allotted for speaking.

In a simple water clock, such as this one from Egypt around 1400 B.C., water flowed out of a hole. The dropping water level gave an indication of how much time had passed.

used gears, wheels with teeth that interlock as they move, to show how the planets and moon moved in their orbits. Eventually, the gears in water clocks also became more complicated. Mechanisms were added that made it possible for a hand to mechanically move around a dial or for chimes to ring.

Some Chinese water clocks were positioned so that flowing water or pouring sand turned a wheel that, in turn, caused a gear to move a hand around a dial. On the dial, markers divided the day into parts but not into hours and minutes as we know them today. At least one Chinese water clock actually divided the day into one hundred even parts, which allowed for more precise timekeeping than most other clocks of the day.

As elaborate as some water clocks were, they were still limited in their ability to keep track of time. One problem

was uneven pace, which meant that no two time periods measured by the clocks were exactly the same. Water dripped more slowly as it emptied from the bowl when the bowl was clogged by mud or pebbles. Weather also affected water clocks. The Chinese found they could keep the water from freezing by adding mercury to their clocks. But in other countries, freezing temperatures made water clocks unusable in winter. So people found other ways of keeping track of time and turned to another one of the basic elements: fire.

Fire

The first person to think of using fire to tell time, according to legend, was King Alfred the Great, who ruled Wessex in England in the ninth century. For many years, King Alfred and his people

Alfred the Great, ruler of Wessex in England in the ninth century, is said to have used candle clocks to remind himself when to pray.

placed when it had burned away. According to legend, the king took one of these candle clocks with him wherever he went.

The Chinese developed an alarm clock that also used fire. The clock consisted of two copper balls that hung by a thread from a horizontal rod. The rod was covered with sticky tar and sawdust. The Chinese lit the tar and sawdust on one end of the rod. When the flame reached the thread, it also burned. When enough of the thread burned away, the balls dropped onto a plate or bowl and the clanging noise woke up anyone sleeping nearby.

Sand

Fire was not nearly as dependable as the sun or water for keeping track of time. Wind and rain could too easily extinguish a fire clock. In addition, fire clocks had one other drawback. They required a constant supply of fuel. When the candle or wood burned completely, the fire clock stopped marking time. Perhaps for this reason, they never became popular. Another type of clock—one that used sand—did catch on, however. A sandglass, or hourglass, had two large glass bubbles connected at the center by a narrow glass tube. At first, these bubbles were made separately and then attached. Later, glassblowers found a way to make a single piece of glass wide, then narrow, then wide again.

Wood or other materials were attached to the end of one bubble to close it off. Sand was then carefully measured into the other bubble. Then, it, too, was covered with a piece of wood so that the sand could not escape. When the sand-

fought with the Danes who inhabited Denmark. During one very difficult battle, the king vowed that he would worship, pray, and serve God for eight hours every day if his troops won. When they succeeded in defeating the Danes, King Alfred kept his promise. He ordered foot-long candles made. Every day, the king worshiped God until two of the candles had burned, which indicated that a period lasting about eight hours had passed.

The candles did not always burn evenly, though. Sometimes, they burned faster because a breeze made the flame hotter. Sometimes, gusts of wind blew out the flame. So to make the candles burn at a more even rate, King Alfred ordered a lantern built of wood. It was shielded at the sides with pieces of thin, clear animal horn. A small door was placed at the side of the lantern so that the candle could be re-

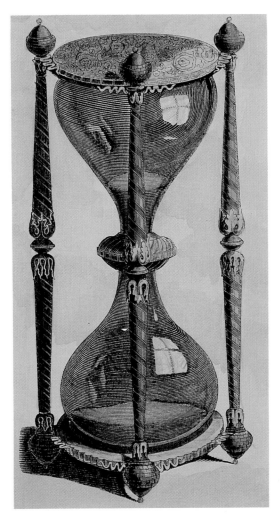

Sandglasses, also called hourglasses, were used to time speeches and sermons. They often featured ornate designs, as does this sixteenth-century French hourglass.

glass was turned on one end, the sand slowly slid into the bottom bubble. When it was turned over, the sand would slowly slide into the other bubble, which was now on the bottom.

Originally, sandglasses were used to measure periods that were longer than a few minutes but much less than twelve or twenty-four hours. Like the Roman water clocks, the sandglasses were used to time speeches and sermons. They were also used on ships to time watch duty, which usually lasted about four hours.

Sandglasses worked well when conditions were right. But things could go wrong. The thin center of a sandglass often became clogged, disrupting the even flow of sand through the glass. And because the sand was coarse, it eventually wore away the glass surface, widening the opening and allowing the sand to flow too quickly. To correct this problem, some sandglass makers replaced the sand with finely ground eggshells. But even then, a steady flow was assured only if the sandglass stood on a perfectly flat, level surface.

The sandglass was the result of the first attempt to build a clock that did not depend on the weather to operate. Gradually, such clocks were developed by horologists, people who study the science of measuring time. But designing improved clocks that could mechanically mark time according to the passage of precisely measured hours and minutes in a day happened very slowly over the next five hundred years or so as people began to see the need for telling time more accurately.

Mechanical Clocks

For many centuries, people used nature and natural elements to help them keep track of time. But nature's clocks were limited in their usefulness. Clocks that depended on warm, sunny weather and daylight, for example, could not be used in the rain or at night. Gradually, people began to desire more consistent and precise methods of telling time.

For this, they would need a mechanical clock. A mechanical clock would run by itself, independent of the natural elements. A mechanical clock would have three important moving parts—an internal or constant power source, something to regulate the pace at which the clock ran, and a way to show what time it was.

Some historians say the first mechanical clocks were in use in ancient China before they appeared in Europe. Once they were developed in Europe, however, sometime between A.D. 1000 and 1300, they flourished. These first mechanical clocks were, for the most part, large iron-framed structures powered by weights. A weight was suspended from a cord. The cord was wrapped

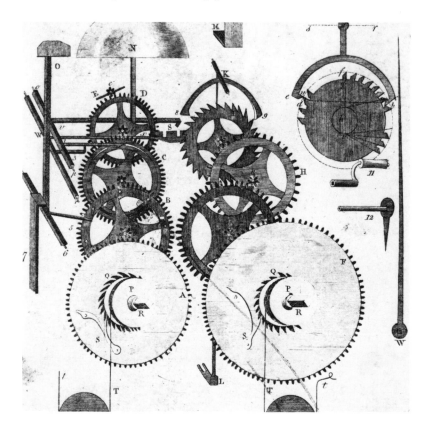

An eighteenth-century engraving depicts the series of toothed, meshing wheels that make up the gear train or clockwork of an early mechanical clock.

be done several times a day. In this way, the weights kept the clock running. But there was no way to be sure it would run at the steady pace needed for telling time accurately.

Controlling the Gears

The man most often credited with inventing the first device that regulated the clock's pace was a French monk named Gerbert of Auvergne. Gerbert was an educated man who had studied math, logic, Latin, Greek, philosophy, astronomy, and music. He also taught at the University of Reims in France. According to historians, while he was at the university, Gerbert probably invented a device called an escapement, which would become the most important part of timekeeping mechanisms until the age of electricity.

The escapement that Gerbert invented interlocked with the teeth of the gears in a clock and controlled the rate at which each tooth was allowed to "escape," or move past, the escapement. An escapement had two short arms of metal that looked a little like an opened staple or the letter *n*. These arms were called pallets. As the gears moved, the pallets slipped between the teeth of the main gear. This slowed the gears down and kept them moving at an even rate. The pace at which the escapement moved determined the speed at which the clock ran.

It is unlikely that Gerbert designed the escapement for a clock that gave the time on a dial as clocks do today. Most early mechanical clocks were designed to drive dials that gave astrological indications and to sound a chime on the hour. But by the 1300s, many me-

Many early mechanical clocks were driven by falling weights, which turned the gears that drove the hands. A fifteenth-century weight-driven clock is pictured here.

many times around a drive shaft, or drum. As gravity slowly caused the weight to fall, the shaft turned and moved a gear known as the main wheel. This gear moved other gears that, in turn, moved the hand or hands on the clock's face. The fallen weight then had to be pulled up by hand so that it could fall once again. Sometimes, this had to

VERGE AND FOLIOT ESCAPEMENT

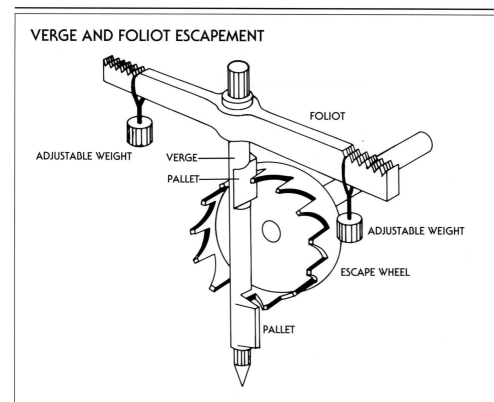

FOLIOT

ADJUSTABLE WEIGHT VERGE

PALLET

ADJUSTABLE WEIGHT

ESCAPE WHEEL

PALLET

Early mechanical clocks were run by falling weights or uncoiling springs. The weights or springs drove a train of wheels, called a gear train or clockwork, that drove the clock. But weights and springs, by themselves, could not keep the gear train running at a constant pace. Weights often fell too fast. Springs lost energy as they unwound. What was needed was a device to regulate the motion of the weights and springs.

In early weight-driven clocks, a verge and foliot escapement accomplished this task. It regulated the gear train through an escape wheel, which was the last and fastest-moving wheel of the train. In the verge and foliot escapement, two pallets are attached to a vertical rod called a verge. As the escape wheel revolves, the pallets catch a tooth on one side and let it escape. Then, the pallets catch another tooth on the opposite side and let it

escape. This alternating action thrusts the pallets first one way and then the other, causing the verge to swing back and forth. This in turn releases the train of wheels in a step-by-step movement.

But even this action can run wild and disrupt the clock's pace. To keep this from happening, another device is added. This device is called a foliot. The foliot is a cross-bar attached to the top of the verge. Two small, adjustable weights hang from each end. The escape wheel now has to oscillate both the verge and weighted foliot, which together serve as an additional check on its movement. Even greater control is possible by moving the foliot weights. This is done by hand. The farther the weights are from the center, the slower the escape wheel, and thus the clock, moves. The closer the weights are to the center, the escape wheel, and thus the clock, speeds up.

chanical clocks had dials with at least one hand that showed the hour.

Some historians think Gerbert designed the escapement for a water clock, and some think he did not make it for a clock at all. Most likely, Gerbert invented the escapement while trying to create a mechanism that would ring bells at regular intervals. These bell ringers had gears that were slowly pulled by weights. When the gears moved far enough, they caused a bell to ring. Without the escapement, the gears might go too fast, causing the bells to ring early, or too slow, making them ring late.

Societies of monks were very interested in telling time. In the Middle Ages, monasteries across Europe were complete communities, with places to make pottery, mill grain, and perform other work. All of these work areas were clustered around a church. The monks who lived there were members of a particular religious organization, and they believed it was important to live by a strict routine and schedule so that they would always be doing useful work and serving God. Bells announced when it was time to pray, work, and worship.

The monasteries were eager to have a better way of knowing when to ring the bells. Therefore, monks talented in mechanics worked hard to invent better clocks. Some of the earliest known mechanical clocks were found in monasteries dating from the late 1200s.

A Better Way

For almost three hundred years, simple escapements were viewed as adequate for controlling a clock's gears and wheels. As a clock ran, though, the teeth of the gears wore down from the pressure of the pallets pushing against them. When the teeth became too worn, the escapement could not control the speed any longer. A better way to control the speed and motion of the escapement and gears was needed. Clock makers then designed new types of escapements or combined the escapement with a regulator.

A regulator is a device that allows for more precise control of the clock's pace. It causes the escapement to tip one way and then the other so that only one pallet at a time touches the gears. When regulators were added to clocks, the escapement's pallets and the gear teeth did not wear down so quickly, and clocks remained accurate for much longer.

The Foliot Balance

It is the movement of the pallets in and out of the wheels in a clock with a regulator that causes the ticktock sound common to mechanical clocks. Weight-driven clocks are designed so that each ticktock lasts one second. One of the first regulators used was called the foliot balance.

Historians are not sure who invented it, but around the end of the thirteenth century, the foliot balance was added to the escapement to improve its control of the pace of the gears and wheels. The foliot balance is believed to have been named after the French word *folier*, which means "to dance about madly." It consisted of two bars put together in the shape of a *T*. Small weights were hung from notches near each end of the bar across the top. The escapement was attached to the middle of the vertical bar, called the verge, next to the main wheel.

When the top bar of the foliot balance swung in one direction, one tooth of the wheel could move away from the escapement. Then, the foliot balance swung back to prevent the next tooth from going too soon. When the bar swung out again, the next tooth was released.

Tower Clocks

The first mechanical clocks to appear outside the monasteries were found in large churches and cathedrals. The weights in one of these wrought-iron clocks weighed several hundred pounds, so the outer frame of the clock had to be tens of feet high to give the weights room to drop. Most of these clocks were placed in a tower that was higher than the building to which it was attached.

Because these clocks were very large, everyone who lived in or traveled through a village that had such a clock could see its large dial and hear the chimes ring. Human clock keepers struck a bell whenever the clock showed a new hour. The word *clock* was taken from the French word *cloche* for "bell."

The tower clocks, once known as great clocks and also turret clocks, appeared throughout Europe between 1300 and 1500. These clocks took a long time to build, sometimes as much as five years. Each iron piece had to be heated in an open forge and hand beaten into the right shape on an anvil by a blacksmith. Then, the pieces were finished by filing. The clock was placed in an open box frame, measuring a few feet across and several feet high. The frame was held together with iron wedges and pins. The first blacksmiths who made clocks lived in France and

Germany, and they were sometimes asked to travel to other countries, such as England, to build clocks.

One of the first tower clocks was constructed in Strasbourg, France, from 1352 to 1354. This clock has been restored and still works. It is as tall as a three-story building and is shaped like a cathedral. It has one dial to show the hours; another to show days, weeks, and months; and a third to show the position of the planets, moon, and sun. It also has a perpetual calendar, which shows the date and important church

The Strasbourg Cathedral clock in France combined fanciful astronomical symbols and a parade of moving figures. An illustration depicts the second of three versions of the now-restored clock.

days and can be used every year.

Many clocks like this one also had figures or puppets made of wood that struck the bell every hour or moved around the dial. These figures replaced the human bell ringers. They were called jacks, possibly after a puppet known as Jack Blandifer on the Wells Cathedral clock made in England in the 1390s. This clock can be seen today in the Science Museum in London.

Many of the jacks were religious figures because church functions were a central part of village life. The clock at Strasbourg, for example, has a jack of Jesus that appears regularly to bless figures of the Twelve Apostles. There are also three wise men who bow before a carving of the Virgin Mary every hour. At noon, a metal rooster crows and flaps its wings.

Guides for Daily Life

Clocks were also built inside European cathedrals. These clocks were a little smaller than those on the outer towers, but they were mechanically similar. They usually had more jacks and frequently had extra gears and wheels that moved dials or spheres to show the church festivals for every year and to show the movements of the planets, sun, and moon.

These religious and astrological events were incorporated into clock mechanisms because they were important to almost everyone. Many people relied on astrology to help them find the best day to plant crops, go to the market, get married, and even have a baby. When a child was born to rich parents, they often paid an astrologer to foretell the baby's future. Religious festivals were also important to most vil-

An illustration of a sixteenth-century French cathedral clock depicts jacks striking bells to sound the hour.

Clocks built inside church cathedrals were often ornate. This clock, built around 1405 in a church in Lubeck, Germany, was destroyed during World War II.

opened and closed. Town councils wanted clocks that would strike the hours that were important to them, which might not be the same as those important to the churches.

Soon, villagers wanted a grand clock for their village square or center to demonstrate their prosperity and artistic interests. Wealthy landowners and noble families wanted to possess clocks, largely because they wanted to be admired for owning such a novelty. Clocks became a kind of popular technological sensation. They were the latest amazing invention. Blacksmiths began to build tower clocks for town halls and palaces. Churches were no longer the only buildings that featured clocks.

Henry De Vick's clock in the Palais de Justice in Paris, France, had a single hand for striking the hour and featured no fanciful figurines. A side view shows the clock's mechanical simplicity.

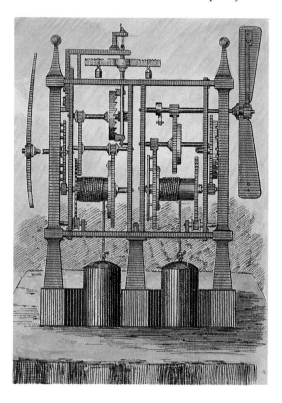

lagers because they were times of worship as well as social events.

As towns and villages gradually grew larger throughout Europe, it became important for each town to have a way to measure time. Unlike farmers, villagers did not decide what to do according to the natural rhythm of the day or season. They needed some way to monitor time throughout the day. Church teachings and the spread of manufacturing work put an emphasis on productivity, or getting a certain amount of work done each day. So people needed to know how much time they had left in a day for finishing their tasks. Village leaders needed to be called together for meetings and to perform civic duties. People had to be notified when markets

One of the most famous clocks of this period was built by a German clock maker named Henry De Vick in 1364. De Vick was ordered to go to Paris by King Charles V of France, who wanted a clock for the tower in the royal palace. For eight years, De Vick lived in the tower and worked on the clock. When he was finally done, De Vick unveiled a clock that was both mechanically and artistically simple.

There were no jacks on De Vick's tower clock, and it had only one dial with a single hand to indicate the hour.

Every hour, a plate under the hand pressed down on a pin that released a rod. Then, the rod hit a bell to tell people the time. Inside, the clock had a simple crown-shaped wheel, called a crown wheel or escape wheel, controlled by an escapement and a foliot balance. This method was the most accurate available, but it was far from reliable by today's standards. Although De Vick's clock was considered one of the best, the time it gave was often two hours off. It has been fixed and updated slightly so that it still keeps time, correctly now, in the

The second of three tower clocks in St. Mark's Square in Venice, Italy, indicates the time and shows the signs of the zodiac and the motions of the sun and moon. In the gallery above the dial, three Magi led by an angel bow before the Virgin Mary. At the top, two bronze giants strike the hours on the bell with their huge hammers. The original clock is thought to have been erected in the 1490s.

Astronomical and astrological events guided the lives of many people, and clocks were built to reflect this interest. The restored sixteenth-century clock at Hampton Court Palace in England depicts the signs of the zodiac and the sun, earth, and phases of the moon.

tower at the Palais de Justice in Paris.

The churches and towns eager to have huge tower clocks usually placed more importance on the decorations than on the mechanics of the clock. Clock making quickly became a creative craft involving skills in metalworking, woodworking, and design. Most Europeans were proud of the beauty and expense of their tower clocks but did not care about their accuracy. These early clocks measured time only by hours, and even then, they were often inaccurate. But this was satisfactory to both horologists and the public.

Clock makers made each tower clock unique by adding different carved religious or military figures and by decorating the dials and hands with gold or silver. Numerous jacks, such as soldiers or knights, were also added to amuse the people. Getting a clock was an important event for a town. Even in prosperous towns, it often took years to raise enough money through taxes and fines to pay for building the clock. In England, for example, a tower clock cost two hundred pounds or more—many times the yearly earnings of a wealthy person. Sometimes, the planning took several more years. Once the clock was begun, it might take another ten years, or even longer, to complete all the handmade parts and decorations.

Although the tower clocks took a lot of time and money to build, villagers expected them to bring increased trade from admiring visitors. When the tower

Human figures called jacks strike the hour and quarter-hour on this fourteenth-century clock in the Church of Notre Dame in Dijon, France.

clock was finished, people from other villages came to see it and, like tourists today, bought local foods and products.

Springing Forward

Although early clocks were usually huge, heavy instruments, some clock makers experimented with smaller versions. But clocks could not be very small as long as they depended on the rising and falling weights that drove the gears. So clock makers explored other possible sources of power for clocks. To make clocks smaller and portable, horologists needed an internal mechanism that was tiny and strong.

Around the beginning of the fifteenth century, clock makers began using springs instead of weights. A spring-driven clock used the energy stored in a coiled spring to move the gears. The mainspring, a thin ribbon of metal, was coiled tightly, with one end attached to the clockwork—a name for the clock's system of gears and wheels—and the other end fastened to the clock's frame. As this mainspring unwound, it moved the clockwork. Locksmiths soon got involved in clock making and helped make the mainsprings. The first clock mainsprings were made of brass, but today they are steel.

Weight-driven clocks were large because the weights needed room to descend. Spring-driven clocks, such as the one pictured below, could be much smaller.

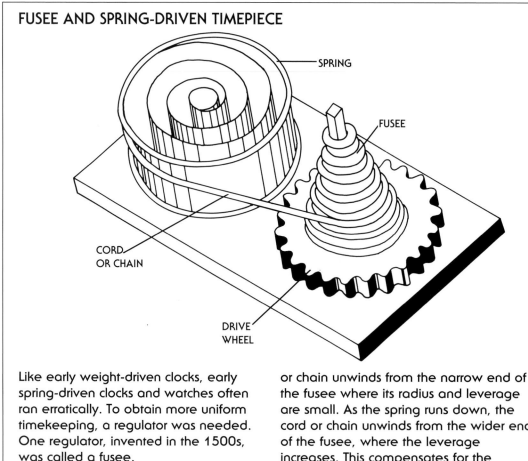

SPRING

FUSEE

CORD
OR CHAIN

DRIVE
WHEEL

Like early weight-driven clocks, early spring-driven clocks and watches often ran erratically. To obtain more uniform timekeeping, a regulator was needed. One regulator, invented in the 1500s, was called a fusee.

The fusee compensates for the changing force of the uncoiling spring. When the spring is fully wound, the cord or chain unwinds from the narrow end of the fusee where its radius and leverage are small. As the spring runs down, the cord or chain unwinds from the wider end of the fusee, where the leverage increases. This compensates for the weaker pull of the spring and keeps the watch or clock running at an even pace.

The major advantage of using main-springs was that clocks could be made much smaller and lighter in weight. Without the addition of long, heavy weights, it became possible to build clocks that were only a few feet tall and, eventually, only a few inches. These clocks were portable and could be used in many places where weight-driven clocks were unsuitable, such as inside homes.

The drawback to spring-powered clocks was that the mainspring did not uncoil at a constant rate, so the clock would run slower as the spring wound down. To make the spring uncoil evenly, an arrangement of gears was added, called a stopwork, a type of which is still used today. What worked even better was a fusee, which was introduced in the first half of the sixteenth century. The fusee was a cone-shaped drum that acted like a reel for a cord attached to the main-spring. As the mainspring ran down, the cord wound around the fusee, keeping the mainspring tension more constant.

Tycho Brahe was an eccentric Danish astronomer who used clocks for mapping the stars.

Spring-powered clocks make a faster ticking sound than weight-powered ones. They usually tick five times per second.

The Minute Hand

Because the timekeeping functions of clocks were usually of secondary interest in the 1300s and 1400s, clock makers continued to make the dials, jacks, and other outer parts of the clocks more elaborate than the inside. Very few of these craftsmen tried to increase the efficiency or accuracy of clocks. The tower clocks, which were at least fifteen minutes slow by the end of the day, were usually adjusted every morning using a sundial. This degree of accuracy was good enough for most people, who relied on the bells heard throughout

the village to tell them the hour. But scientists, especially astronomers, needed a more accurate clock to help them study the stars.

Tycho Brahe was an eccentric Danish astronomer who spent most of his life in the 1500s observing and mapping more than seven hundred stars. He invented several instruments to help him find stars and record their paths across the sky. Using an instrument with a sighting device on it, he could find out how high a star was. Then, he used a clock to determine how long it took for the star to pass a point in the sky,

Brahe frequently complained about the inaccuracy of his clocks. His complaints may have led to the addition of a minute hand, possibly like the one in this sixteenth-century clock.

known as the meridian, so he could compare it to a star he already knew about, such as the sun.

Clocks that measured only hours were too inaccurate for Brahe's needs. Counting out the seconds and minutes was not much better. Brahe complained to everyone, including a German named Jost Burgi, who built clocks and other instruments. Trying to help Brahe, Burgi may have been the first person to add a minute hand to a small clock. The earliest reference to a minute hand is found in Brahe's journals for 1577. Only a few years later, in 1581, he mentions a second hand. Despite Burgi's help, Brahe and other astronomers were still not satisfied. Brahe complained in 1587 that he could not get his four clocks to agree on the time and still used a clepsydra, or water clock, when he wanted accuracy.

Despite the dissatisfaction of Brahe and other astronomers, most people grew more enthusiastic about having clocks. Village leaders ordered decorative minute hands added to some tower and cathedral clocks. The clocks still ran from fifteen minutes to several hours slow by the end of the day, but few people cared as long as the clock was impressive to residents and visitors. The mechanics of the clock had changed little in the three hundred years since the foliot balance was invented. But, after about 1600, more attention would be paid to making clocks do a better job of telling time.

The Pendulum

The discovery that brought a greater degree of precision to timekeeping came about almost by accident. In the

The pendulum made clocks more accurate than ever before. A reconstruction of Christian Huygens's seventeenth-century pendulum clock is shown here.

1500s, a young Italian medical student named Galileo Galilei noticed a lamp swinging in a church. Timing it with his pulse, he found that each swing took the same amount of time regardless of the distance the lamp traveled.

Galileo was so fascinated by the lamp's constant swinging motion that he conducted various experiments in hopes of learning more. During the course of these experiments, he obtained the same results over and over again. When a weight was suspended from a fixed point so that it could swing freely under the action of gravity, its swinging motion remained constant. This device came to be known as a pendulum. Galileo, who later made some of the world's most important findings in astronomy, tried to use the pendulum in clocks, but did not succeed. About one hundred years would pass before another scientist would figure out how the pendulum could be used to run a clock.

In 1656, a Dutch astronomer named Christian Huygens learned how to use a pendulum to control the pace of the clock. Huygens was a talented scientist who began in childhood to study physics, mathematics, optics, and astronomy. He figured out many of the principles of these sciences and in-

Huygens's success in applying pendulums to clocks impressed clock makers of the day. Dutch clock maker Jan Van Call built this clock, one of the first pendulum clocks, in 1657.

vented and refined devices, such as a lathe and optical lenses, that depended on understanding these principles.

Huygens wanted to invent a clock that would help ships navigate at sea. He did not succeed. But he did succeed in adding the pendulum to clocks, and his work proved to be one of the greatest advances for telling time on land. The type of pendulum Huygens used for a clock regulator was a long, thin, lightweight metal rod with a heavier round plate, called a bob, at the bottom. To make a pendulum regulate a clock-

Huygens wanted to invent a clock for telling time at sea. Instead, he greatly advanced the accuracy of clocks used on land.

PENDULUM AND ANCHOR ESCAPEMENT

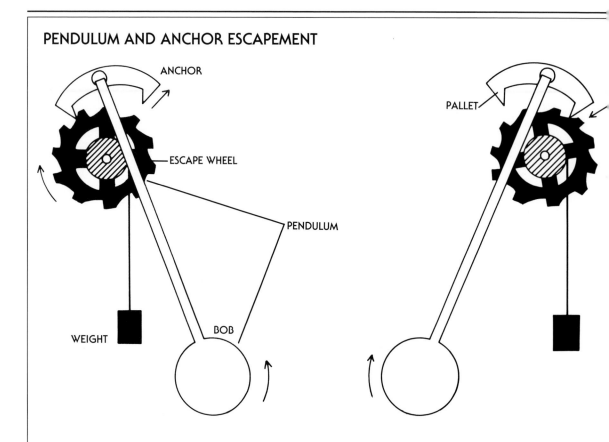

The addition of pendulums to clocks in 1656 made timekeeping more accurate than ever before. As long as the pendulum swung freely from a fixed point, receiving a slight push at regular intervals, it maintained a constant motion under the force of gravity.

Many pendulum clocks are driven by a falling weight. As the weight descends, the gears turn. The turning gears move an escape wheel, which is itself connected through gear trains to the hands of the clock. The swinging

pendulum and anchor escapement regulate this motion to help the clock maintain a steady pace.

As the pendulum swings, it rocks the anchor back and forth. The anchor pallets alternately engage the teeth of the escape wheel, releasing one tooth on each side with every swing. This action checks the motion of the escape wheel and gives the pendulum a slight push that keeps it swinging. The escape wheel then turns the hands of the clock.

work, Huygens knew he would have to shape the pendulum just right so that it would swing back and forth at exactly the right speed. He worked out a mathematical formula for the shape of the bob and the length of the pendulum's rod.

In weight-driven clocks, when the pendulum swung left, the left pallet on the escapement released a tooth on the main wheel. When it swung to the right, the right pallet released another tooth.

The pendulum proved to be a bet-

Huygens presents a pendulum clock to French king Louis XIV.

ter regulator for clocks than a foliot balance. Pendulums could be made to swing at a very exact rate, which would stay constant. They did not slow down nearly as soon as the foliot balance and the mainspring did. Therefore, clocks with pendulums would run correctly for a much longer time. Instead of running at least fifteen minutes slow each day, clocks with a pendulum usually lost only ten seconds a day.

Another advantage of pendulum clocks was that they could run for a much longer period of time. Since the pendulum's swinging motion depended on gravity, rather than on a force within

the clock, pendulum clocks ran without needing daily winding. Although these clocks eventually needed to have their springs wound or their weights pulled up, most went for more than twenty-four hours and some lasted for eight days before needing to be started again.

Even with this newfound technology, clock makers still devoted most of their attention to ornate designs and intricate decorations. These features intrigued the wealthy at first and later captured the hearts of the working classes. By the 1600s, clocks were spreading throughout Europe, and by the 1800s, they seemed to be appearing everywhere.

CHAPTER 3

From Town Squares to Living Rooms

In the 1600s, many of the aristocrats buying tower clocks for their palaces and castles decided they wanted personal timepieces to display indoors as well. The use of springs to power clocks made smaller clocks possible, although they were still very expensive. Especially in Great Britain, kings and rich landowners bought these smaller clocks as a symbol of their wealth and importance.

The decorations on these household clocks were much simpler than those on the clocks in cathedrals and towers. One type of household clock that gained early popularity in Great Britain was shaped like a bird cage. It was usually hung on the wall like the lanterns used during those days. Elaborate brass work was featured between the domed top and the square bottom of these bird cage or lantern clocks. The clock maker often put his trademark or the buyer's coat of arms on the brass work. Sayings or mottoes were sometimes etched into the brass sides of the clock as well.

Many of these bird cage clocks were powered by weights. The clock needed to be about nine feet high to give the weights room to drop slowly. Every time the clock ticked, the weights dropped a little bit. Two or three times a day, a servant had to pull down the cords attached to the weights to lift them back up.

Sometime around 1665, an unknown clock maker decided to put a

Grandfather clocks found a place in many households as treasured pieces of furniture.

Some household clocks contained animated figures and became a form of entertainment for the wealthy. This chariot clock, made around 1600 in Augsburg, Germany, was intended to perform on a long banquet table.

long, wooden case around these weights and the pendulum. The case could stand on the floor. Known then as a long-case or coffin clock, this type of clock was designed during a period of great development in British furniture making. The long-case clock kept time fairly well and was created as a beautiful piece of wooden furniture. This style of clock later became known as a grandfather clock about 1876 when a popular song used the expression "my grandfather's clock."

As household clocks became more common, both makers and buyers began to enjoy more elaborate designs. Particularly in Germany, people liked so many extra functions and figures that household clocks were more like fancy toys than tools for timekeeping. One

popular style of clock was shaped like a small castle with the dial in the middle for the time. It also had dials that showed the phases of the moon; the position of the sun and moon in relation to the zodiac signs; the position of the sun, moon, and some stars in the sky; and the day of the month.

Entertaining Clocks

People admired the clever clock designs and jacks on the big tower clocks, and they urged clock makers to add similar amusing movements to their household clocks. On small clocks, movements like this are called automata. Some could be quite elaborate.

One German clock was shaped like

Soldiers pace back and forth in front of a castle atop the dial on this clock built in Germany's Black Forest area around 1800.

a pyramid, with a carousel near the top. In the back, just below the carousel, a piece called a plane reached to the bottom of the clock. It was angled like a slide and had a groove down the middle. A small ball was released at the top, went down the groove into a cup at the bottom, and then was shot back up by a trigger-release mechanism. This trip took the ball one minute. Every three hours, the knights and soldiers on the carousel paraded around a figure in a turban who pounded on a drum with hammers in his hands. The dials near the bottom were less interesting and showed the hour, the date, and the day of the week.

One of the most famous clocks with automata was made by the Englishman James Cox around 1750 for the Russian statesman Grigory Potemkin. Now in a museum, this large clock has been

named the Peacock Clock. The clock is shaped like a tree stump and has ivy, mushrooms, and gourds made out of porcelain around the bottom. A mechanical cricket hops around and chirps every second. On the lower branches, a squirrel chatters, a rooster crows, and a caged owl sings. In the higher branches, a life-size peacock moves about, showing its beautiful feathers. The clock dial is hidden inside a mushroom. It did not matter that the dial was not easy to find because it was less important to Potemkin and his friends than the entertaining automata.

The interest in amusing clocks probably inspired the first cuckoo clock, which was built by Anton Ketterer around 1730 in southern Germany. Ketterer did not use any metal pieces. Since he lived in the Black Forest, he used wood to make his clocks. Like the earlier bird cage clocks, cuckoo clocks hang on the wall and need room for the weights to drop. The square cases are made of wood with carvings of leaves, birds, and small animals attached. Above the dial, a small door opens every hour or half hour to let a wooden cuckoo bird come out to chirp the time. Eventually, many of these clocks were made with more elaborate automata.

Household Clocks

Clocks moved from the public square into the private home for a number of reasons. Society in Europe and America was changing during the sixteenth and seventeenth centuries. Towns were growing into busy marketplaces, and more people were becoming educated. In these towns and cities, a middle class made up of people neither very wealthy

Cuckoo clocks originated in Germany's Black Forest area in the 1700s. This early cuckoo clock has a hand-painted wooden dial.

man beings could accomplish with their time. As business practices became more sophisticated, the notion that "time is money" arose. Even religion, particularly the Protestant churches that emerged during the sixteenth century, emphasized that people should be useful and productive and not waste time. Clocks helped people measure how they were using their time so that they could discipline themselves to be more efficient.

In the seventeenth century, clock makers began to make clocks that did not have to hang on walls or stand on the floor. These clocks could sit on a table or a shelf. In Great Britain, table clocks, or bracket clocks, were especially popular. Many of these table clocks had the same design as the tower and long-case clocks but on a smaller scale. Soon,

nor very poor developed for the first time. This class included merchants, lawyers, doctors, druggists, and others who earned a comfortable living and could afford decent houses, good clothes, and a few luxuries. These people bought clocks because they liked them and could afford them. The middle class got used to seeing clocks and soon figured out that business could be run more efficiently when everyone in a community had the same way of measuring time.

Historian David Landes in his book *Revolution in Time* explains that with clocks in their homes, people could control their use of time. The Renaissance, a period from about 1300 to 1700 in which knowledge, invention, and creativity expanded very rapidly throughout Europe, taught the value of what hu-

An elaborately carved wall clock encased in delicately chiseled silver represents clock making during the Renaissance.

With his mass-production methods, Eli Terry made inexpensive clocks in the early nineteenth century.

best clock makers hired experts to do each job: one to cut the wheel, another to build the case, another to shape the dial, and so on. The whole process usually took several months. For this reason, clock makers usually did not start making a clock until someone had ordered it. Repairs also took a lot of time because broken parts had to be built from scratch by hand, just as the originals had been.

The expertise and time required for making clocks and the cost of these clocks meant that each clock maker could sell only a few. So most clock makers worked at other jobs. They were often blacksmiths, gunsmiths, and locksmiths while pursuing the clock-making craft.

a dome-shaped top with a carrying handle was devised.

As clocks became more ornate and complicated, their builders had to be more skilled. They needed special training in how to work carefully with the metals. They needed to learn how to cut and form the delicate pieces, how to attach them, how to oil them so they ran smoothly, and how to repair them. Clock making grew into a highly skilled occupation. Gradually, certain European cities developed reputations as clock-making centers. Among these were Paris, London, Stockholm in Sweden, and Geneva in Switzerland. Each country began to develop its own style of clock design. To become an expert clock maker able to build a clock alone, a young person was apprenticed to a master for several years.

Through the 1700s in Europe and colonial America, clocks remained expensive because each one had to be completely handmade. Some of the

Inexpensive Clocks

Eli Terry was a talented young American who did not want to do anything except make clocks. To earn a living at clock making, though, he would have to sell a lot of clocks. Around 1800, he came to the conclusion that more people might buy clocks if they could see them already built. He made some samples and rode his horse around the New England countryside, showing his clocks to farmers. Although people admired Terry's clocks, most could not afford them. They cost about twenty to forty dollars, which was as much as the average farmer earned in about two months.

Terry then realized that it was expense, not lack of interest, that was preventing people from buying clocks. He believed that if he could find a faster and easier way to make clocks, then he could sell them at a cheaper price and more people would buy them. Terry's

MECHANICAL CLOCK

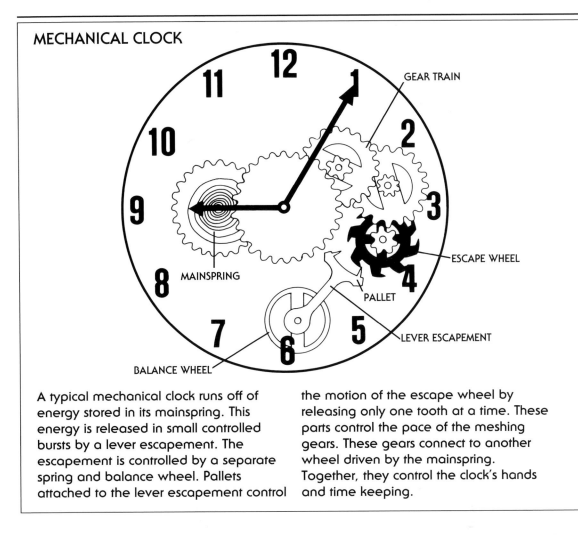

A typical mechanical clock runs off of energy stored in its mainspring. This energy is released in small controlled bursts by a lever escapement. The escapement is controlled by a separate spring and balance wheel. Pallets attached to the lever escapement control the motion of the escape wheel by releasing only one tooth at a time. These parts control the pace of the meshing gears. These gears connect to another wheel driven by the mainspring. Together, they control the clock's hands and time keeping.

search for a way to do this led him to investigate the machines being used to make rifle parts. These machines could make parts much faster than people could by hand.

Terry decided to build similar machines for making clock pieces quickly. Each machine would produce a different part of a clock. One machine might make the wheels, another the spring, another the case, and another the dial, for example. When the parts were done, Terry or one of his assistants put them together in a clock, while the machines made more parts. All the parts used were identical and would fit in any of the clocks. If a clock broke and needed a new piece, Terry had one ready.

He opened his first factory in Connecticut in 1803. At first, Terry made grandfather clocks with his mass-production methods. Within a few years, however, he was also building smaller household clocks. These clocks had a pendulum and weights, a dial with both hour and minute hands covered by a glass door, and lovely carvings or paintings. Terry charged only two dollars for some of his clocks, so almost anyone could afford one. By 1808, his factory was so successful that he was producing more than eighty clocks a month, and by 1822, he was making six thousand clocks a year.

Other people copied Terry's methods, and many clock factories opened in New England and Europe during this time. These factories made simple, inexpensive clocks in many different styles. In the United States, some of the most popular manufactured clocks were shaped like banjos, lyres, and other musical instruments. Since these clocks were produced quickly by machinery, rather than slowly by hand, they cost only about five dollars. Almost everyone could afford to spend a week's pay, or less, on the attractive clocks. As more and more people bought household clocks, the clocks lost the prestige associated with objects that only the wealthy could own. But they gained tremendous popularity.

In the 1800s, there were only a few mechanical changes in clocks and these changes slightly improved accuracy. Clock makers also began to use brass instead of wood for clock frames. For the most part, however, clocks changed little, but they did become more affordable. Clocks began to appear in homes at many more economic levels. As a result of seeing so many clocks, people gradually became interested in making better use of them. For that to happen, clocks had to be more convenient to use and they had to tell time even more accurately.

Electric Clocks

Mechanical clocks were immensely popular, but they could be bothersome to operate because they had to be wound

Banjo-shaped clocks, like this one made by famed clock maker Simon Willard in the early 1800s, became popular in the United States.

by hand to run. Although no one realized it at the time, the electrical experiments being run by European scientists during the nineteenth century would change this situation. In 1800, an Italian scientist named Alessandro Volta designed an electric battery by placing pieces of zinc and copper in a salt solution. Other European scientists improved on this idea over the next forty years. They used electric power for many different purposes, including to jar the needle of a compass and to control the needle of a telegraph.

In 1840, a Scottish scientist named Alexander Bain decided to try using an electric battery to run a clock. After twelve years of experimenting, Bain finally created the first electric clock. It had an electromagnet attached to the bob on the end of a pendulum. An electromagnet is a core of magnetic material surrounded by a coil of wire. An electric current is passed through the wire to magnetize the core.

Bain affixed two other magnets to the inside of the clock, one to the left and one to the right of the bob. These magnets pulled the electromagnet on the bob. First, the bob went left, then right, then left again, and so forth. This was called the master clock. The vibrations from this clock produced electric impulses that were sent to another clock. This second clock was called a slave clock because it did not have its own source of power. Every second, the hands on the slave clock were moved by the electric impulses from the master clock.

Bain and the men who later improved on his master clock were scientists. They were more interested in in-

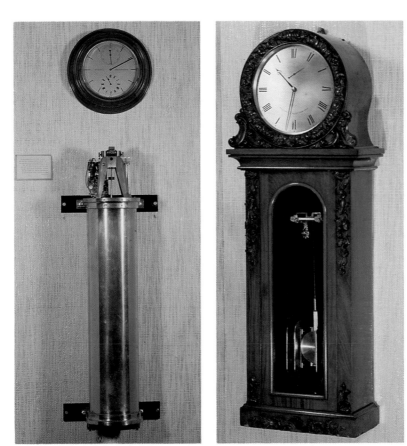

Scottish scientist Alexander Bain opened the way for others who saw the value of electric clocks. Clock maker W. H. Shortt built this master and slave clock (far left) in 1922.

creasing their knowledge about physical forces, such as electricity, than in the practical applications of their discoveries. More than seventy years passed before Henry Warren, an American inventor, tried to develop electric clocks that everyone could use.

The Warren Clock Company

Warren was mechanically minded even when he was very young. As a boy, he designed a small motor run by gasoline to operate his mother's sewing machine. He got his first patent when he was only twenty-three for the Thermophone, an instrument that measured temperature at a distance. When he was much older, Warren started his own company called the Warren Gear Works. While working with different types of gears, he became interested in clocks. By 1912, his interest in clocks had grown so much that Warren decided to devote his time to them and even changed the name of his business to the Warren Clock Company.

Using the ideas of Bain and others, Warren developed an electric clock run by batteries. These clocks were attractive, but they were very expensive and broke easily. So Warren began to build a clock that would not need batteries. The new clock he envisioned would operate with the normal electric current being sent to more and more households. Like Bain's clock, it would be a slave clock, with the power coming from an outside source of electricity instead of from an electromagnet.

At the time, alternating electric current was sent in cycles through wires to each home from an electric company. Inside the house, this power was re-

ceived as waves of electricity. It was sent to households at a standard rate of sixty cycles, or waves, a second.

Warren put a small motor inside a clock and plugged it in. The motor turned a series of gears that made the hands of the clock move. The motor was coordinated to match the electric company's standard sixty cycles a second so the gears would move at the correct speed.

Warren connected the clock to the power supplied by the Boston Electric Company to see if it worked. The clock ran on the electric current, but it was inaccurate. It was at least ten minutes off each day. After examining the clock and motor thoroughly and finding

American inventor Henry Warren tried to develop practical electric clocks. He built this electric battery pendulum clock around 1915.

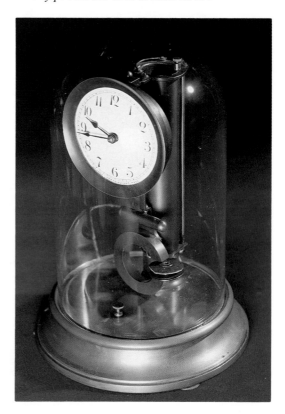

nothing wrong, Warren decided to measure the electric current. He discovered that the electric company was inaccurate. Although the companies claimed to send current at a standard rate of 60 cycles a second, the actual current varied anywhere from 25 to 125 cycles per second. Sixty cycles a second was an average, not a constant, rate. The rate varied because there were no government regulations about the rate at which power must be transmitted and because electric companies were changing their technology rapidly and still experimenting with different ways of operating. Until the electric companies acknowledged and corrected this problem, no clock using household alternating current could keep accurate time.

Warren knew that by himself, he could not convince the electric companies to maintain a standard current. So he concentrated on making better clocks that ran with electric batteries. Within a few years, the Warren Clock Company was so profitable and well respected that the influential General Electric Company became one of Warren's partners.

Eventually, with the help of General Electric, various industries were persuaded that maintaining a standard sixty cycles of electric current a second would benefit them. An accurate master electric clock could be used to regulate the speed of the machines used to make silk and paper, for example. This consistency would eliminate or reduce the flaws in the product and increase the workers' efficiency. When these and other manufacturing industries joined General Electric to request that electric current be supplied at a constant sixty cycles a second, the electric companies eventually complied.

Electric clocks using this current could finally keep accurate time. This standard also meant that people could plug a clock in and it would keep running, as long as the electric company did not have a power failure. For most people, the biggest advantage of these clocks was that they were automatic. They did not need to be wound every day or even every week.

In a short time, electricity made clocks more useful than ever, and the demand for them in homes, in public buildings, and in business increased. Because of electricity, in less than a century, more changes were made in the mechanics of clocks and more uses found for them than during the previous nine hundred years since Gerbert's first escapement. Today, clocks are everywhere. But nowhere, perhaps, have people been affected by clocks as much as they have in the workplace.

Clocks in the Workplace

Since the earliest days of mechanical clocks, people who own businesses have used clocks to help them control the time their employees spend working. On farms, peasants simply toiled from sunrise to sunset. But as more people began to live in towns and as industry and trade developed, this natural way of beginning and ending the day did not work. Inside buildings, more signals were needed to tell workers when to start and end work and when to break for meals. Town officials needed to know when to open and close the town gates and marketplace.

The textile industry in medieval Europe was the first to use time signals. The owners of these businesses hired many people to weave or dye cloth or to do other work in their own homes and cottages. Town authorities agreed to ring bells from the church tower or the village square to tell workers in these "cottage industries" when to start work,

Clocks, along with other technological advances, led to changes in work habits. The workday in a turn-of-the-century textile mill, as in other factories, ran according to the clock.

when to eat a midday meal, when to return to work, and when to quit for the day. These work bells led to some conflicts. The employer did not always trust the workers, whom he could not see, to work as much time as they were told. And workers did not believe the employers always rang the bells at the right time.

Clocks helped resolve this conflict. Chiming clock towers provided regular signals on the hour or on the half and quarter hours. When chimes could be heard and dials could be seen, everyone knew what time it was and agreed that the clock was correct.

Clocks in Factories

By the eighteenth century, manufacturers in America and Europe were very interested in being able to measure the efficiency of their businesses and their potential for making profits. To do this, they needed to know how much work was being done during the day. The cottage manufacturing system became more frustrating for employers. They decided to bring workers together into a central workplace where they could see their workers' activities. The technical innovations brought about by the Industrial Revolution made this centralized system common beginning in about the 1770s.

Over the next two centuries, industry became an increasingly bigger part of the economy, especially in Europe and the United States. In 1850, for example, about three out of every four Americans worked on farms. By 1920, farming had become so unproductive and expensive that half of all Americans had moved to the cities, and many of them worked in factories. Factories had steam and electricity to power their machines for hours at a time. Factory owners had clocks to tell their workers when to arrive and when to leave.

More and more, the workday was measured by the clock. By 1920, factory workers were spending about ten hours a day, six days a week at their job. The Crucible Steel Company in Midland, Pennsylvania, was typical. Workers arrived at the gate at 6:30 in the morning. Workers spent five hours operating their equipment. At noon, a whistle blew and the workers had an hour to eat lunch and relax. At 12:55 P.M., a warning whistle sounded. All workers were expected to be back at their place before 1:00 P.M. Five hours later, at 6:00, a whistle signaled the end of the workday. Employers reprimanded and fined workers who were late. But good workers who arrived on time often received a favorite prize — a clock!

Automatic Time Clocks

Clocks influenced factory work in other ways, primarily by measuring the number of hours and minutes a person had worked and would be paid for. In 1895, an American inventor named Willard L. Bundy built a time clock that printed the exact time a worker arrived and left. In factories using this time clock, each worker was given a numbered key. When the workers arrived, they put their key into a slot in the time clock. The number of the key and the time it was inserted in the clock were printed on a piece of paper. Cards later replaced the keys.

Many workers hated the time clocks. They felt the factory was a prison and

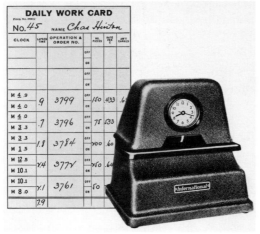

some way to outsmart the newest time clock, but, in the end, technology would prevail. Advancing technology led the industrialized world toward a new concept of time that focused on the relationship between time and production, or how much a worker could accomplish in a given period of time.

Motion and Time Studies

Owners of businesses felt they had to get the most production possible out of every hour a worker was being paid. The more accurate clocks of the late nineteenth century soon developed into specialized timekeeping devices that measured workers' productivity. Under the direction of experts who understood how to time actions to a fraction of a second, timekeeping technology enabled employers to measure

the clock a guard. So they found ways to fool the time clock and the boss. Some workers discovered they could blur the time printed on their cards by inserting them just as the clock was changing to the next minute. This made it difficult to tell what time the worker arrived or left.

Various improvements made it more difficult for workers to tamper with time clocks and their time cards. An enterprising worker could nearly always find workers' output and plan how a factory could most efficiently operate. Clocks made businesses much more aware of productivity while providing a way to measure it.

In 1881, Frederick W. Taylor, an American engineer, began doing time studies for industrial businesses. His career in time studies began unintentionally. Taylor worked in the machine shop at the Midvale Steel Company in Philadelphia. When he became foreman, he concluded that many things could be done faster and better. The president of the company gave him permission to study two of the best workers to find out exactly what qualified as a good day's work. Taylor wanted to discover how much a worker could accomplish during each day over a long period of time.

Taylor studied the machinists and timed how long various tasks took them. He used this information to teach the managers how to accurately plan how much time workers would need for the different tasks to be accomplished. By planning ahead and by letting the workers know exactly how long each task was expected to take, the managers were able to make the workers more efficient.

Searching for Productivity and Savings

After that first study, Taylor never went back to being a foreman. Instead, he began to conduct time studies for various companies. In 1898, Taylor studied workers shoveling coal and iron ore at the Bethlehem Steel Works in Bethlehem, Pennsylvania. He wanted to determine the most efficient method of shoveling to save the company money.

Frederick W. Taylor was one of the first people to conduct time studies for businesses interested in increasing productivity.

He discovered that workers usually lifted about 3 1/2 pounds of coal at a time but could lift as much as 38 pounds of iron ore with each shovelful. Taylor decided to study this further.

Taylor chose two of the best workers and gave them large shovels at first, then gave them smaller and smaller ones. He had the men shovel many different types of coal and ore. Taylor's two assistants timed the men with stopwatches and kept track of how much they shoveled. Taylor noticed that if the workers shoveled too much coal in a single scoop, the extra weight slowed them down. If they shoveled too little coal in a single scoop, the job took longer and the workers seemed unchallenged. By comparing time and motion, Taylor discovered that the workers performed best when they lifted 21 1/2

Lillian Gilbreth studied physical processes in an effort to increase worker efficiency.

pounds of material with every scoop.

Taylor used this information to design a large shovel for lighter material, like ashes, and a small shovel for heavier material, like ore. With these new shovels, the workers could lift exactly 21 1/2 pounds of material. By using these new shovels, the company got the most out of its workers and saved money.

Efficiency Experts

As the idea of worker efficiency, or productivity, began to take hold in American industry, researchers conducted more studies. American engineers Frank and Lillian Gilbreth decided to study the physical processes involved in different types of work rather than the overall time required to complete a task. They hoped to develop more efficient ways for workers to complete their tasks in less time.

To begin, Frank Gilbreth studied

how different men laid bricks when they built a wall. He noticed that because of the tools and workplace conditions, the workers made many unnecessary and time-consuming movements. This prompted him to redesign the scaffold on which the bricklayers stood to work. He also taught the workers how to use fewer movements to accomplish each step of the job. In this way, Gilbreth increased the number of bricks a worker could lay in an hour from an average of 120 to an average of 350.

With his wife Lillian, Gilbreth analyzed workers in other industries. They determined that the process that made the bricklayers more efficient could be applied to other workers as well. A worker in any field could accomplish more work in less time if the work process involved fewer movements, shorter

Frank Gilbreth taught workers how to accomplish tasks with fewer movements.

reaches, and the use of both hands. These kinds of worker efficiency improvements would save almost any company money, and this appealed greatly to business owners. Time-motion studies caught on quickly in the manufacturing and business worlds, especially in the United States. Factory owners, in particular, realized they could use the results of these studies to teach workers the most efficient way to do a given job.

Time-motion studies also helped owners design the factory for less waste of worker time. In addition, the studies helped develop the concept of a fair day's work for both worker and employer and introduced the idea of higher pay as an incentive and reward for faster work. Partly as a result of studies like these, the working day was gradually shortened from 10 to 8 hours. It was found that workers were most efficient with a workday of that length.

Factory owners also used the information from time-motion studies to develop timed assembly lines. Up to this point, in most assembly processes, workers stood at tables and each gathered all the parts needed to assemble a product.

Time and motion studies contributed to the development of factory assembly lines. Assembly lines attempted to make human work patterns as predictable as clocks.

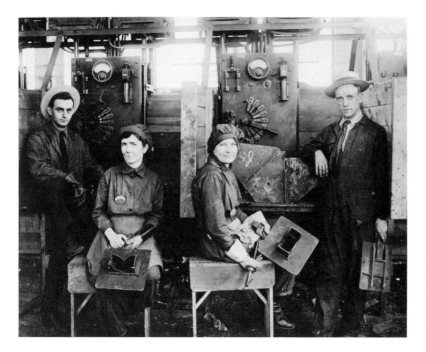

Many shipyard welders and other workers switched from twelve-hour shifts to eight-hour shifts during World War I.

The process was slow and irregular. On the new assembly lines, however, workers stood near a moving conveyor belt. Parts to be assembled or inspected passed by the workers at a set speed. Slow workers had to speed up to keep pace with the assembly line. Fast workers who sometimes sacrificed quality for speed had to slow down. In this way, factory owners got the most out of their workers in the least amount of time possible. In many ways, the assembly line was an attempt to make human work patterns as regular and predictable as the workings of a machine, such as a clock.

Shift Work

With assembly lines to keep work moving at a steady pace and plenty of available workers, factory and business owners began to see the benefits of operating all day and night. Some factories and mills, for example, have equipment that must be kept running all the time. Others have furnaces or forges that take a long time to cool down or heat up again, so it is easier and cheaper to keep them going.

Clocks, along with electric lights and machine tools, made it possible to keep production going by having workers on the job up to twenty-four hours a day, in different shifts. No longer was daylight necessary for work. When factories first began using shift work, employees worked on either a day shift or a night shift that was twelve hours long. By 1918, when the United States became involved in World War I, shift workers usually worked for eight hours at a time. At that time and again when World War II began, the government's demand for weapons and other products caused many munitions and airplane factories to convert to a shift system. By 1945, when World War II ended, many other factories had become aware of the benefits of shift work and employees were used to the idea of working this way.

Since then, other kinds of businesses have also offered twenty-four-hour service by employing people on shifts. Telephone operators, disc jockeys, news announcers, pilots, flight attendants, train engineers, and security guards usually work in shifts. The emergency services of fire departments, police departments, hospitals, and ambulance companies are frequently provided by employees whose shifts last longer than eight hours.

Four-Day Workweek and Flextime

Today, both workers and employers are keenly aware of how much time workers devote to their job. Since the 1970s, some business owners have realized that work time can be divided in ways other than the eight-hour shift, five days a week.

Some companies are willing to change from the standard eight-hour shift because employees are demanding more choices about how much time they spend at work, at leisure, and in meeting the responsibilities of home and family. Some observers believe alternatives to traditional work hours will allow each individual worker to schedule work time according to his or her "internal" clock, the body's natural increases and decreases of energy throughout the day. Another reason for these changes in the workday is that different people perform best on different schedules. By allowing employees to develop their own schedule, business owners can increase their productivity.

One innovation in many industries is allowing people to work for ten hours a day, four days a week. Another option is flexible time, or flextime. Generally, flextime allows workers some choice over which hours they work as long as they work eight hours a day or forty hours every week. New kinds of time clocks have been developed to keep track of employees on flextime.

Clocks helped create the modern concept of time as the way to measure productivity in the workplace. Clocks were an important part of the changes that made our society more industrialized and urban. One of those changes was the creation of faster, more reliable means of transportation. Clocks had a very significant role in that process.

Clocks Move the World

When the first sailing ships began crossing the world's vast oceans in the 1400s, captains and crews had little to guide them on the often treacherous journeys. These early sailors relied mainly on the movements of the moon, sun, and stars to help them find their way. Gradually, they developed other navigational tools. But even these were limited. Moon tables and star charts guided sailors at night. Compasses pointed the way north, and sextants measured the sun's distance above the horizon. Together, these tools enabled sailors to determine their latitude, or how far north or south they had traveled from the equator.

But even with a compass or sextant and various tables, sailors could not determine longitude, or how far east or west they had traveled. This is because the measurement of longitude, unlike latitude, required an accurate timepiece. Longitude is measured by dividing the globe into 360 equal north-to-south strips called degrees. In 1520, the Flemish astronomer Raimer Gemma Frisius proposed a method for determining longitude based on his knowledge that the earth rotates 15 degrees per hour or a full 360 degrees in twenty-four hours. So if a ship's navigator knew what time it was on the ship, he could

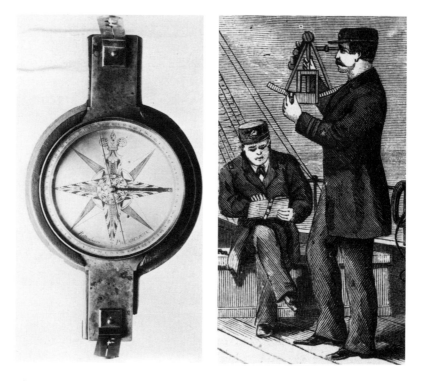

The compass (left) and the sextant (right) were essential tools that allowed sailors to navigate at sea. But these two instruments could not tell sailors all they needed to know.

compare that time to the time at a common reference point from which longitude was measured. The difference in time would show how far east or west the ship had sailed. The sailors could tell what time it was on the ship by the sun's position. But without a clock, there was no way to know the time at the reference point. No one had invented a reliable clock for telling time at sea.

Another complication was that there was no common starting point for this measurement. Everyone used the equator to measure latitude, but navigators and mapmakers of different countries determined longitude according to an important landmark in that country. A map for French sailors, for example, usually listed Paris, the capital of France, as zero degrees longitude.

To navigate, most early sailors resorted to a method called dead reckoning. Each day, they guessed how fast they were going and used a compass to try to keep on course. They also guessed which way the winds and currents had sent them and hoped they were right. Dead reckoning was not a very good way to navigate. Many ships lost their way, and many journeys ended in shipwreck. The key to improving navigational techniques lay in finding a way to accurately determine longitude, and the key to determining longitude hinged on having a clock that would work at sea.

Greenwich Observatory

Among those searching for a way to measure longitude at sea was Great Britain's King Charles II. King Charles ruled at a time when ships of many European countries were heavily in-

Great Britain's King Charles II desperately sought a way for his ships to accurately determine longitude.

volved in exploration, colonial expansion, and trade. Great Britain had a large navy and huge shipping fleets, and the king knew that faster and more accurate ships would bring his country greater riches.

With that in mind, King Charles built an observatory in Greenwich, England, in 1675. The task of the Royal Observatory was to "perfect the art of navigation" by preparing lunar tables. King Charles believed, mistakenly, that longitude could best be determined by observing the path of the moon relative to the positions of certain stars. Astronomers of the time favored this method over the one suggested by Frisius.

But telling longitude by astronomical tables did not work well, and navigators again became interested in the method that would require a clock. Gradually, through the 1700s, navigators and mapmakers came to agree that Greenwich should be the reference point, or prime meridian, from which all calculations of longitude would be made. What they needed was a clock that could be set on Greenwich time before a ship set sail. This clock would have to stay accurate without being affected by the movements of the ship, the weather, or gravity. At the time, no such clock existed. Unknown to the rest of the world, however, such a clock was being created by an Englishman named John Harrison.

The Marine Chronometer

Harrison was a carpenter who taught himself how to build clocks. He knew that prizes of money were being offered by several countries, including Great Britain, to anyone who could discover

John Harrison spent much of his life inventing a clock that would tell time at sea. His marine chronometer gave sailors the tool they needed to pinpoint their locations.

an easier, more accurate way to determine longitude. In Great Britain, the largest prize would be given for a method that was accurate to within thirty miles when tested on a voyage to the West Indies. Since the average British worker earned less than two hundred pounds a year, the twenty-thousand-pound grand prize was more than most people made in a lifetime. Intrigued by this challenge, Harrison made many different drawings of a timepiece that he thought would work at sea. He planned to take his sketches to London to show them to the Board of Longitude.

In 1728, on his way to London, Harrison stopped at the Greenwich Observatory to ask for advice from the respected Astronomer Royal, Edmond Halley. Halley was impressed by Harrison's designs but thought the Board of Longitude would want to see more than drawings before it awarded any money. Halley sent Harrison to visit George Graham, the best clock maker in London. After talking about Harrison's plans all day, Graham agreed that an actual timepiece, not just designs, was needed. Graham even loaned Harrison some money to help him make a timepiece to show the Board.

Harrison's First Marine Clock

Harrison, working with his brother James, finished his first navigational clock in 1735. Today, these clocks are called marine chronometers. This first marine clock weighed seventy-two pounds and was kept in a case two feet long and eighteen inches wide. It was mounted sturdily so that the sway of a

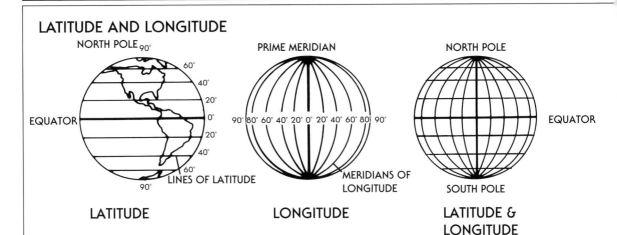

LATITUDE AND LONGITUDE

LATITUDE

LONGITUDE

LATITUDE & LONGITUDE

For many centuries, sailors had no reliable way to determine longitude, or how far east or west their ships had sailed. They had tools for determining latitude, or their north or south position. But to accurately determine longitude, they needed a clock that would keep time at sea. This clock was invented in the 1700s. With the addition of the clock, sailors could accurately determine both latitude and longitude, the grid coordinates that can be used to locate any point on the earth.

Latitude describes a north or south position in relation to the equator. All points on the equator have a latitude of zero degrees. The North Pole has a latitude of ninety degrees north and all points between the equator and the North Pole lie in the northern latitudes. The South Pole has a latitude of ninety degrees south and all points between the equator and the South Pole lie in the southern latitudes.

Longitude describes the east or west position of a point on the earth's surface in relation to an imaginary line called the the Prime Meridian. Like the Prime Meridian, which runs through Greenwich, England, the lines of longitude run north and south along the earth's surface. Most countries have agreed that Greenwich lies at zero degrees longitude.

ship would not interfere with its time-keeping. It had four dials to show seconds, minutes, hours, and days. Like most other clocks of the time, gears turned the hands on the dials and pendulums controlled the pace of the gears.

But Harrison's clock differed from the others in at least one important respect. Harrison built his pendulum with alternating rods of iron and brass in an arrangement called a gridiron. Most pendulums had been made of wood or brass or iron alone. But Harrison knew

that those materials expand or contract in heat or cold. This expanding and contracting action changes the shape of the bob or the length of the pendulum rod, which would change the pace at which the pendulum swung. As a result, the pace of the clock was altered.

Harrison realized that changes in temperature were an inevitable part of life at sea and that the changes might be even more drastic than on land. So his only logical option was to find another material for making the pendulum. He settled on iron and brass, thinking the expanding and contracting of the two metals would offset each other. When the iron contracted in response to changes in temperature or humidity, the brass would expand. Since these two forces counteracted each other, the whole gridiron pendulum would keep swinging at the same beat and the clock's accuracy would not be affected by changes in the weather.

A year later, the Board of Longitude agreed to let Harrison test his chronometer on a round-trip voyage to Lisbon, Portugal. The ship's navigator made his calculations in the usual way with a compass, sextant, and astronomical charts. Harrison used his chronometer to track the ship's speed and distance from Greenwich. As they returned to England, the captain and the navigator were certain they were approaching the Start River. Harrison determined that they were about ninety miles west of the Start. Harrison's figures were accurate. The chronometer had kept time much better than anything tried before and made far more accurate navigational calculations possible.

Harrison Builds Three Others

Although the marine chronometer amazed the ship's captain, Harrison was not completely satisfied. He was a perfectionist, and he was sure he could make an even better chronometer for the longer trip to the West Indies. He

Harrison's first navigational clock (below) weighed seventy-two pounds. Later models were much smaller and lighter. Harrison's Number Four chronometer (right) worked better than all the rest.

finished a second chronometer, called Number Two, in 1739. It was stronger and slightly smaller than the first chronometer. Great Britain and Spain were at war, however, so no one wanted to risk trying Number Two on an actual sea voyage. While he waited for the war to end, Harrison worked on a third, even better chronometer, which he finished in 1757.

While building Number Three, however, Harrison came up with some new ideas for a much smaller, lighter chronometer. The Board of Longitude gave Harrison a little more money so he could finish this smaller one. Board members planned to send both on the test voyage to the West Indies.

Finally, in 1760, Harrison finished Number Four. It looked like a big, thick watch and was only five inches in diameter. It had one dial, which had three hands to show hours, minutes, and seconds. Since it was so much smaller than the first three chronometers, it was much more portable. Harrison built a plain wooden box to go around it. He was so sure that Number Four would keep accurate Greenwich time that he decided to drop Number Three from the test altogether.

Number Four Succeeds

In November 1761, Number Four went on a test voyage to Jamaica. Harrison, then sixty-seven years old, sent William, his son and assistant, to use the chronometer on the five-month-long voyage. When the ship reached Jamaica, it had missed its destination by only one mile, according to William Harrison's calculations with Number Four. The chronometer had run only about five

Frustrated over prize money denied him for his successful chronometer, Harrison sought help from Great Britain's King George III.

seconds slow. Household clocks that stayed on land were seldom as accurate.

Despite this amazing accomplishment, the Board of Longitude refused to pay Harrison the large prize. Some members of the Board wanted to win the prize themselves, so they said the test was inconclusive. They gave Harrison some money and told him more tests were needed. Four years later, after several successful tests, the Board told Harrison to build a copy of his Number Four chronometer. The Board planned to test both, it said, in a variety of temperatures. But after Harrison and his son finally finished Number Five in 1771, the Board decided to use someone else's copy of Number Four for the tests instead.

Harrison was so angry that he asked for a special meeting with King George III. Harrison told the king how he had spent the past forty years building an

A stone plaque marks the Prime Meridian at Greenwich, England, the agreed-upon starting point for determining longitude and time.

accurate chronometer and how the Board of Longitude was denying him the prize money. The king spent ten weeks testing Number Five. The chronometer was only four seconds fast, which meant it would be about a mile off at sea. The king agreed that Harrison deserved to win the prize, but the Board still would not pay him. Finally, Harrison begged Parliament for the prize money. The king and Parliament both told the Board to pay Harrison. Harrison was an old man of eighty when he finally got the prize money. He died only three years later in 1776.

The marine chronometer created by Harrison was a great help to sailors of all countries. They finally had an accurate way of determining their longitude and no longer had to risk landing in a strange place, not finding land at all, or wrecking on rocks because they were lost at sea. Although many people tried to improve on Harrison's Number

Four, few succeeded. Only minor changes, mostly to the spring and balance, have made the marine chronometer more accurate.

Greenwich was the reference point for determining longitude, and by 1848, Greenwich time had been adopted as the standard time for most of Great Britain. Within a few years, signals telling Greenwich time were sent every hour, on the hour, through the switching station at London Bridge to the Electric Telegraph Company's central station. From there, they were transmitted to other telegraph stations, railroads, and post offices. For the first time, one clock was being used to tell time throughout an entire country.

Still, most of the smaller towns and villages in Great Britain and in other countries continued to use "local" time. This local time was determined by the sun. When the sun was directly above the town, the village clock was adjusted to read noon. As the sun moved westward, though, it was directly over each town a few minutes later. When it was noon at one place, it would be a few minutes after noon in the town to the east.

Trains

In the United States, time differences were unimportant to most people until trains began to carry the mail around 1840. Since the days of stagecoaches, the mail had been delivered to each town according to a strict schedule. People eagerly looked forward to the arrival of the mail at a certain time each day. Each stagecoach, and later each train, even had a postal guard who carried a gun and an official pocket watch to make sure the mail arrived on schedule.

As trains became faster and went to more towns and cities, it was possible for people to make business appointments in other towns. More people began to travel, and they found that keeping track of each local time was confusing and difficult. Passengers who traveled from Portland, Maine, to Buffalo, New York, for example, found that their watches were thirty-five minutes off when they arrived in Buffalo. This meant that passengers frequently missed their train connections or had long waits.

In the late 1800s, there were about seventy different time zones in the United States. Trains became a more common form of transportation for freight as well as for mail and passengers. The confusion and inconvenience of using local times now affected everyone—people sending or receiving packages and mail, people expecting visitors arriving by train, and passengers trying to catch a train. As more people depended on knowing the accurate arrival and departure times of trains, the railroads began to develop timetables. But these tables frequently were almost impossible to read because they tried to list all the different local times someone might want to use.

Some railroad lines tried to make things simpler by having their own "standard" time, usually based on that of the main city on the line. But this only added to the confusion. By 1880, some railroad stations displayed several large clocks in an attempt to help their passengers. In the station at Buffalo, for example, three different clocks showed local times in Buffalo, New York City, and Columbus, Ohio. Yet train travel continued to be a frustrating experience for many travelers. They often missed their connections simply because the railroads operated according to different clocks.

Time Zones

An American educator named Charles Dowd thought the jumble of local times was not only confusing but unnecessary.

A hodgepodge of local time zones complicated train travel. Passengers frequently missed train connections or had long waits.

WORLD TIME ZONES

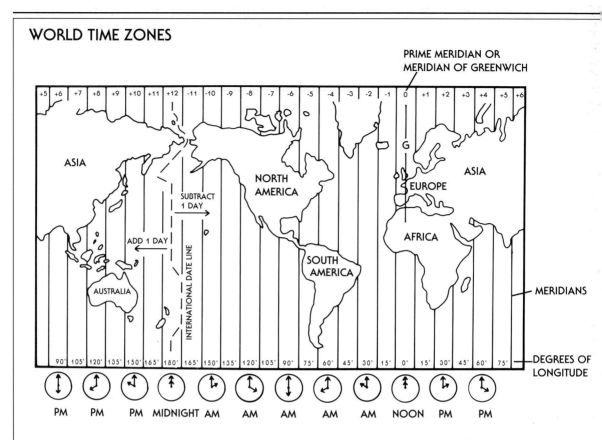

Before the adoption of international standardized time zones, clocks around the world were set to hundreds of different local times. As world transportation and communication systems became more complex, this patchwork of local times became especially confusing and difficult.

Most people today recognize and use 24 time zones. All places within a given zone use the same time and each zone is one hour ahead of or behind its neighbors. This system enables a person to determine the time almost anywhere on earth.

The time zones are based on the earth's natural rotation. The earth makes one complete rotation every 24 hours. All 360 degrees of the earth's circumference also pass beneath the sun once in 24 hours. Because it takes one

hour for the earth to travel 1/24 of 360 degrees, or 15 degrees, a new time zone begins every 15 degrees.

The time zones are marked by imaginary lines of longitude called meridians. Meridians run north and south along the surface of the earth, from the North Pole to the South Pole. The meridian that runs through Greenwich, England, serves as a common starting point for determining time and east and west directions. The Meridian of Greenwich, also known as the Prime Meridian, is located at 0 degrees longitude. Halfway around the world, at 180 degrees longitude, is the International Date Line. These two lines mark the world's two halves or hemispheres and they are exactly 12 time zones apart. This means that when it is noon at Greenwich, it is midnight at the International Date Line.

In 1869, he developed a simple plan to eliminate the problem for the railroads. Since the United States covers about sixty degrees of longitude, Dowd proposed that the country be divided into four time zones of about fifteen degrees each. At every fifteen degrees longitude, or about 750 miles, a new time zone would begin. Since it takes the earth about one hour to rotate over fifteen degrees longitude, each time zone would differ from its neighbor by an hour. The imaginary time zone lines would be adjusted a little so they did not go through the middle of any cities.

For several years, local communities resisted Dowd's proposal. But in 1883, the railway managers met in Chicago and accepted Dowd's plan. All railroads, post offices, and many towns in the United States and Canada began using standard time, as it was called, on November 18, 1883.

Agreeing on Greenwich

The next year, representatives of twenty-six countries met in Washington, D.C., for an International Conference on Time. When the meeting ended, they had agreed that Greenwich, England, should be considered zero degrees longitude (which mapmakers and many ships' navigators had decided long ago) and that world time should start there (which the United States time zone plan already assumed). Taking Dowd's idea a step further, the rest of the world was divided into twenty-four time zones of about fifteen degrees longitude each, beginning at Greenwich. At noon, Greenwich time, the time zone directly east of Greenwich, which includes parts of Africa, Europe, and Scandinavia,

would be one hour later, or 1:00 P.M. Traveling west of Greenwich, the next time zone is one hour earlier than Greenwich time, or 11:00 A.M.

By 1900, this system of time zones was in use in Great Britain, the United States, and many other countries. It was formally adopted by the U.S. Congress in 1918. With only twenty-four international time zones, the local times of hundreds of places had to be adjusted. Towns where local time was ahead of the new standard time had to set their clocks back. Places where local time was earlier than standard time had to put their clocks ahead.

At first, many people objected to the new time zones. Some believed that God had determined the original time and that standardizing times would be contrary to his plan. Others thought they were actually losing or gaining time. Some people simply disliked the

Charles Dowd developed a simple plan for coordinating time zones in the United States.

World time zones simplified international transportation, communication, and commerce. The clocks pictured here tell the time in various cities around the world.

idea of conforming to an international standard. And a few protested because they were sure the whole idea had been thought up by clock makers who would be paid to readjust clocks all over the world.

Within a few years, though, people in almost every country realized how much easier it was to have standardized time zones. The advantage of this system is that a person can figure out exactly what time it is now or what time it will be later anywhere in the world.

Standardized time zones have made the scheduling of modern ships, trains, buses, and airlines much easier, and

clocks still play an important role in navigation for both airplanes and ships. Since the 1950s, transmitters and satellites have been used to send carefully timed signals based on sophisticated clocks to help aircraft and ships stay on course.

For ships, the three most widely used systems are called Loran-C, Omega, and Navstar. In these systems, pulses or radio signals are sent to ships from stations throughout the world or from satellite transmitters. The signals are based on a very sophisticated clock located at the U.S. Naval Observatory in Washington, D.C.

With the receivers located on ships and aircraft, navigators can determine the exact time a signal arrives and can receive hundreds, even thousands of signals at a time. While the ship is in port or the aircraft on the ground, the navigator adjusts the receiver to the correct longitude and latitude. Then, when the ship is at sea or the plane in the air, the receiver can automatically translate the time signal transmissions into the correct longitude and latitude. This system functions much as Harrison's chronometer did two hundred years ago, but it is completely automatic and far more accurate as a navigational tool.

Clocks changed not only public life by helping modern transportation systems to develop but also influenced people's private lives. No longer the prized possessions of only the wealthy, clocks are now commonplace, everyday items that people carry with them wherever they go.

Watches—Clocks That Travel

In the sixteenth century, European clock makers began to build table clocks for use in homes. Some of these clocks came with a special box so they could be carried when the owner wanted to take them on a trip. Soon, clock makers built even smaller clocks that could be carried on a chain around a person's neck or waist. These personal clocks were much bigger than watches of today. They were made of iron, and some were

Early watches were mostly drum-shaped boxes, usually heavily gilt and with a single hand for telling the time. Sometimes they are called clock-watches because of their size and weight. The clock above was made in 1560 by a German locksmith named Hans Gruber.

so heavy that a servant was hired to carry it as the owner went around town.

The First Watch Is Crafted in Europe

The first of these early, portable time-pieces that could truly be worn by a person was built in 1504 in Nuremberg, Germany. Its creator was a young locksmith named Peter Henlein. Henlein worked on this first watch for two years. He completed it under the supervision of a church abbot who had given him sanctuary from an angry mob. The mob had unjustly accused Henlein of thievery and murder.

Under the abbot's guidance, historians believe, Henlein crafted the world's first watch. It was neither accurate nor attractive. Henlein's drum-shaped time-piece, built entirely from iron, was held together by pins and rivets. It stood six inches high, had only one hand to mark the hours, and had no crystal to cover the dial. A coiled iron mainspring made the watch run. But without any way to control the spring's power, the watch was hopelessly inaccurate. When the watch was fully wound, the spring pushed the lone hand so quickly around the dial that it often gained as much as an hour within the first hour or two. As the spring unwound, its force lessened and the hand slowed down and lost more time than it had gained.

In addition, Henlein tried to regu-

late the watch's pace with an old-fashioned foliot balance, which brought only limited success. The watch kept adequate pace when it lay on a table and the foliot balance could swing horizontally. But when the watch was carried, the foliot balance swung vertically and the pace changed.

Despite these problems, Henlein is credited with making the first watch because it was he who found a power source for a portable timepiece that could be worn. But their inability to control the spring, and thus regulate the clock's pace continued to puzzle watchmakers. A Swiss clock maker, Jacob Zech, came up with one idea. In 1525, some historians say, Zech invented a crude, though fairly effective device for controlling the mainspring. He called it a fusee. The fusee was a cone-shaped, grooved spindle that looked something like a top. The spindle acted like a reel for a strand of catgut that Zech attached to the main-

A sixteenth-century engraving (above) depicts work in a clock maker's shop.

Watches known as Nuremberg eggs (left) became popular fashion accessories. Some had intricately designed cases and dials.

spring. As the mainspring ran down, the catgut unwound toward the larger end of the spindle. This kept the tension on the mainspring more constant even as it wound down.

A Craft Grows

With these advances, watchmaking began to grow as a craft in parts of Europe. At first, watchmaking was concentrated in Germany, England, and France. But as watchmakers moved to other countries and as word of new developments spread, clock makers, blacksmiths, and jewelers throughout Europe began to make watches. By 1550, Geneva, Switzerland, had distinguished itself as a watchmaking center. Its reputation grew as goldsmiths and metalworkers migrated from neighboring countries. These immigrants became known for producing highly decorative watches, as did the city they decided to call home.

Although many watchmakers tried to combine the new mechanics with intricate designs, others focused their attention on the decorative outsides. One Nuremberg watchmaker, for example, made a crude watch from a fashion accessory popular with both men and women of the time. This watch, called a Nuremberg egg, resembled the egg-shaped, scented musk balls fashionably worn around the neck or waist. It included none of the recent mechanical advances that made watches more accurate. But its decorative porcelain case and unique shape made it a popular item with wealthy Germans and, eventually, with other wealthy Europeans.

Early watches with unusual shapes won some powerful admirers. In the 1600s, Mary, Queen of Scots, had a

Mary, Queen of Scots, is said to have had a watch set inside a case shaped like a skull. Skull watch pendants, like this one from about 1640, became popular items.

watch set inside a case shaped like a skull. To see the dial, she turned the skull upside down and the jaw opened. Other watches were shaped like books, flowers, crosses, stars, or animals. Many

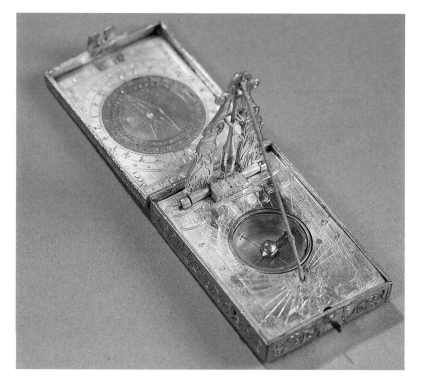

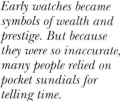

Early watches became symbols of wealth and prestige. But because they were so inaccurate, many people relied on pocket sundials for telling time.

were covered with gold, silver, crystal, or other costly materials. Some had scenes from mythology, religion, or nature painted on the cases. Watchmakers found other ways to impress and attract wealthy customers. They crafted watches that could be worn as a bracelet or a ring in addition to those worn as a pendant around the neck. Women often spent a lot of time choosing watches to match their different outfits. Although men initially also wore these fancy watches as decorative accessories, they soon began hiding their watches from view. They may have wanted to keep them protected from thieves. Or they may have decided that plainer, less decorative watches were more manly. Whatever the reason, watchmakers began styling simpler watches for men. They also made them thin enough to fit in a man's vest pocket.

Watches, like clocks, became sym-bols of wealth and prestige because only the rich could afford them. Yet their importance as actual timekeeping pieces was secondary to their role as fashion ornaments. A person who really wanted to know the time usually carried a pocket sundial or listened for the sounds of town criers or chiming tower clocks.

The Balance Spring

For watches to become more than mere ornaments, someone would have to find a way to make them more accurate and convenient to use than a pocket sundial. For this, watchmakers turned to clocks. The seventeenth-century idea that made clocks more accurate than ever was the pendulum. Its free-swinging motion remained constant under the force of gravity and therefore pro-

MECHANICAL WATCH

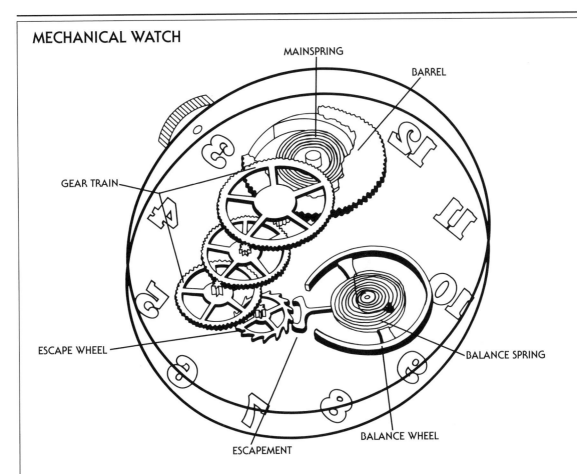

The driving force behind a basic mechanical watch is a mainspring. The mainspring is coiled inside a hollow barrel. As the spring unwinds, it turns the barrel. The rotating barrel, which is toothed and geared, drives the wheels of the watch that make up the gear train. Energy is transmitted through these moving wheels to an escape wheel. The motion of the escape wheel is controlled by an escapement, which in turn is regulated by a balance spring and balance wheel. The job of the escape wheel is to limit the release of energy to small quantities at exact intervals so that the hands move at the correct speeds.

vided a reliable way of controlling a clock's pace.

Applying this same principle to watches posed a problem for two main reasons. Portable timepieces were not large enough to contain free-swinging pendulums and the pendulum needed to swing from a fixed position. Watches were to be worn and their movement would disrupt the pendulums' swing. What was needed was a regulator as reliable as the pendulum that could also work undisturbed by motion.

This achievement occurred around 1660 or 1675, with the invention of the balance spring or hairspring. The identity of its inventor is disputed. Some historians give credit to Christian Huygens,

A drawing depicts watchmakers hard at work at the Elgin National Watch Company founded in 1865 in Illinois.

the man who adapted pendulums to clocks. Others say the famed British scientist Robert Hooke invented the balance spring. In all likelihood, both men were working on the idea. It was Huygens, however, who introduced the new device to the world of watchmaking at just the right time.

The balance spring is a thin spiral spring attached to the staff of a balance wheel, which swings first one way, then the other under the tension of the spring. A regulator shortens or lengthens the spring to alter its tension. This, in turn, controls the swings and, ultimately, the accuracy of the watch. The first balance spring was made from a pig's bristle. Later, other materials were used to control the balance wheel at better and more predictable rates. But

for its time, the early balance spring was the best idea yet for improving a watch's ability to keep time.

A period of great inventiveness followed in which various people continued to refine the internal mechanisms of watches. By the early eighteenth century, the basic mechanical parts had all been invented for a standard watch. Yet the world still lacked a truly accurate pocket watch or wristwatch. Further refinements would finally make this possible. But the cost of owning such a watch remained an obstacle to all but the wealthy.

In 1720, for example, a watch cost as much as the average servant earned in ten years of work. Even during much of the 1800s, watches were designed with royalty and the wealthy classes in mind. The more novel the watch design, the more interest it sparked. John Arnold, a famous British watchmaker, designed a watch especially for King George III during this time. The watch, set in a pinkie ring, was smaller than any other watch made up to that time. The Russian empress, Catherine the Great, was so impressed with Arnold's work that she requested a similar watch for herself. Knowing the value placed on a finely crafted, one-of-a-kind watch, Arnold refused.

Although not every watch made during this time had the unique character of the Arnold watch, they were still all made by hand. And although handcrafted watches took time to make, they were being made in ever greater numbers. In 1687, for example, Swiss watchmakers built five thousand watches. By 1799, watchmakers in Geneva were turning out fifty thousand watches annually. Most of these watchmakers still worked out of their homes and spent several weeks making just one watch.

Gradually, though, European watchmakers began to specialize in making individual watch parts that could then be assembled at a central location. It was around this time, in the early and mid-1800s, that American watchmakers also turned to the idea of mass-producing watches. Mass production would bring changes in the quality and character of watches, and it would mean that almost anyone could afford a watch.

Building an Affordable Watch

One of the many companies that tried to manufacture a more affordable watch was the Elgin National Watch Company, founded in 1865 in Elgin, Illinois. The factory hired expert craftsmen and manufactured its first watch in 1867. But the watch cost $117, plus the price of a covering case. Since the average person earned only about $1 a day and had to support a family of six or more, only the rich could afford it.

Some clock makers kept trying to create a pocket watch that everyone could buy. The first person to succeed was Daniel Buck, a watchmaker in Massachusetts. He spent months designing an inexpensive watch. The Benedict and Burnham Manufacturing Company in Waterbury, Connecticut, gave him money and space to build the watch. In

An early Waterbury watch advertisement. The Waterbury watch was among the first affordable pocket watches.

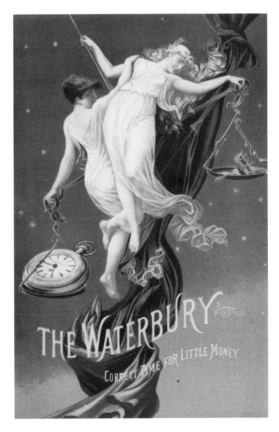

1880, Buck produced a pocket watch that sold for only four dollars. He called it the Waterbury watch. The price of the Waterbury made it a popular item, especially with shop owners who gave them as gifts to good customers.

The dial of the Waterbury watch was a piece of paper glued to the inside plate of the case. Mechanically, the watch used an old-fashioned mainspring and escapement. But winding the watch took about 140 turns, and this led to many jokes about the watch and the winding it required.

Nevertheless, the Waterbury inspired other ideas. A Michigan businessman, Robert Ingersoll, bought thousands of Waterbury watches for eighty-five cents apiece in 1892. He then sold them for one dollar through a mail-order catalog. People all over the country

An illustration shows the internal mechanism of a Waterbury watch.

The Waterbury's popularity blossomed when Robert Ingersoll began selling them through mail-order catalogs and advertising in newspapers.

bought the cheap pocket watch for their friends, their children, and themselves. For twenty-five years, the Ingersoll Dollar Watch, as the watches came to be known, was usually the first watch a young person owned.

Wristwatches

By 1900, almost every American man and boy owned at least one pocket watch, but very few had a wristwatch. Wristwatches were considered fancy bracelets and worn mostly by women.

But World War I, which lasted from 1914 to 1918, changed this attitude. There were no pockets on a military uniform for a pocket watch. If a soldier found a place to carry his pocket watch, it was usually hard to reach during fighting. American soldiers who fought in Europe found that French, British, and German soldiers wore wristwatches instead of pocket watches.

American soldiers praised the European wristwatches in letters home. Soon, soldiers heading for Europe were receiving wristwatches as going-away presents and quickly learned to like them. When the war ended, the Americans brought many European wristwatches home. These timepieces quickly became popular. The fad became a lasting fashion, replacing pocket watches as an item in most wardrobes.

American, Swiss, and other companies began manufacturing wristwatches in large quantities. Rapid changes made the watches more convenient and accurate. Now, watches are among the most frequently manufactured items in the world. Today, more than half a billion watches are made each year, and 300,000 are sold every day in the United States. The first change that made watches so popular was that they became self-winding.

Self-Winding Watches

Self-winding watches became popular around the same time as wristwatches, although they had actually been created much earlier. Swiss and French watchmakers had attached a small pendulum inside a pocket watch as early as 1770, hoping the pendulum would keep a watch running just as it did a clock. The results were disappointing. To work properly, a pendulum needed to swing freely from a fixed point. This was difficult in a movable watch.

In 1923, a British watchmaker named John Harwood decided to try this idea again. But instead of using a tiny pendulum, Harwood attached a small weight to the center of the watch. This weight moved whenever the wearer moved his or her arm, such as while walking. The weight was connected to a series of gears to increase its force. The mainspring was wound by the normal movement of the wearer's arm. The force of the weight on the gears kept the watch going even while the wearer rested. People liked these watches because they did not have to remember to wind them every day or two.

The Inexpensive Timex Wristwatch

At first, like early pocket watches, wristwatches were expensive. They were built slowly and carefully with high-quality components. A man named Joakim Lehmkuhl created the first inexpensive wristwatch in 1949. Lehmkuhl was born in Norway but fled from the German Nazis to the United States in 1940. He had college degrees in science and electrical engineering but was more interested in being a successful businessman than a scientist. He joined the Waterbury Clock Company and became its president in 1942. Fifteen years later, the company was renamed the United States Time Corporation, and he became its chairman.

Lehmkuhl realized, as Ingersoll had, that more people would buy watches if they cost less. He was determined to produce an inexpensive wristwatch. Using cheaper materials than the traditional steel, Lehmkuhl developed a wristwatch called the Timex. It was attractive enough for the average person and kept time to within a minute or two

The Timex wristwatch was advertised as waterproof and able to withstand the shock of a pounding horse's hoof.

each day. While its style and accuracy were inferior to some of the finely crafted European wristwatches, it had one big advantage: it cost only about eight dollars. By this time, even the least expensive watches made by other companies cost at least thirty dollars.

Within a few years, the Timex had another selling point: durability. The Timex was built to withstand both normal and unusual shocks a wristwatch might encounter while being worn. Sales representatives demonstrated the strength of a Timex by hitting the watch on counters. They showed customers that the watch was waterproof by plunging it into a pail of water. On television commercials, a Timex wristwatch was fastened to a horse's hoof, the propeller of a ship, and even to a high diver. People all over the world liked these inexpensive, durable watches so much that they were buying about thirty-one million Timexes a year by the time Lehmkuhl retired in 1973.

Electric and Electronic Wristwatches

The Timex and all other wristwatches were wound by hand or were self-winding. Winding was not necessary with the first electric wristwatch, which was developed by the Hamilton Watch Company of Pennsylvania. In 1957, this company began selling a watch that was run by a small battery. The battery, about the size of a shirt button, transmitted enough power to operate the balance wheel, which controlled the hands. This electric watch was more accurate than any other wristwatch and would last at least one year.

A few years later, a Swiss electronics engineer named Max Hetzel developed the first electronic watch. This watch had about half the moving parts of a normal watch. Its battery powered a transistorized circuit, a compact device that controls the flow of electric current that runs the watch. In place of the usual escapement, to regulate the watch's pace, Hetzel used an inch-long tuning fork. He chose this two-pronged instrument because he knew that it produces vibrations at a predictable frequency.

A small mercury battery sent power through an electronic circuit to two magnets, one near each side of the tuning fork. The magnetic force caused the tuning fork to vibrate exactly 360 times each second. These vibrations were transmitted to the balance wheel and moved it at the rate of about once a second. The moving wheel, in turn, caused the hands of the watch to move at the correct speed.

Although Switzerland was recognized as the watchmaking center of the world, Hetzel could not convince any of the Swiss watch companies that his idea would successfully produce an elec-

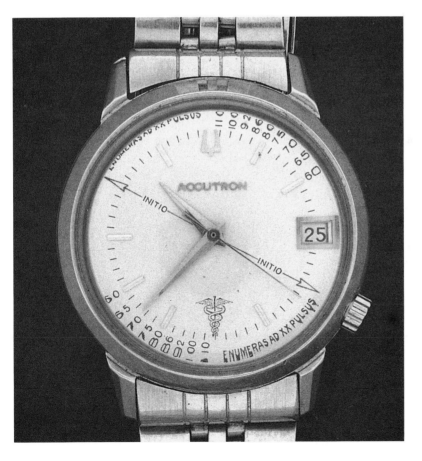

The Accutron electronic wristwatch had about half the moving parts of average watches. It supposedly never lost more than a minute a month.

tronic watch. So he traveled to the United States. The Bulova Watch Company of New York decided to take a chance and began selling the watch in 1960. They called it Accutron and guaranteed that the watch would never lose more than one minute a month. The Accutron was so successful that many Swiss watch companies regretted that they had not listened to Hetzel. Some even paid Bulova for the right to produce a similar watch.

The Swiss were dismayed at falling behind. So they established a special research laboratory, called the Centre Electronique Horologer (CEH), to develop an even more precise way to tell time. Within a year, in 1961, the CEH had found a way.

Quartz Crystals

The CEH researchers knew that anything that moves at a uniform rate can be used to regulate a clock. They also knew that quartz, when cut carefully, vibrates at a constant 100,000 times a second. The CEH decided to test quartz as a means of achieving greater accuracy in a watch. To do this, CEH researchers cut the quartz, connected it to batteries, and inserted these in marine chronometers. When tested, the chronometers ran more accurately than any mechanical or electronic timepiece yet created. When rating a timepiece, a score of 0 is perfect accuracy. The best mechanical timepiece scored 2.8. The quartz chronometers, though, scored 1.2. But these chronometers were large and used a lot of energy. The batteries had to be changed every week.

Over the next six years, the inventors tried quartz crystals in a variety of timepieces. They continued to reduce the size and amount of energy used. At the same time, accuracy improved until one timepiece achieved a nearly perfect rating of 0.0099 in 1967.

Unfortunately for the Swiss, they had spent too much time on research and not enough time watching their competitors. Less than a year after the CEH revealed its test version of the electronic quartz-crystal watch, a Japanese company called Seiko produced a similar, less expensive model. The Seiko watch had a tiny battery that caused a quartz crystal to vibrate 32,768 times each second. The quartz was shaped like a tuning fork, as in Hetzel's first electronic watch. The vibrations were counted by an integrated circuit, called a chip, and relayed to the hands to move them around the dial. A good quartz-crystal watch lost only about one minute a year.

Digital Wristwatches

Only a few years later, in the early 1970s, two more advances in watchmaking occurred. With these advances, a timepiece was made that did not need hands or a dial. At the same time the CEH was developing quartz-crystal timepieces, researchers in other fields were creating tiny computers using electronic circuits and transistors. In 1970, the Hamilton Watch Company put quartz crystals and miniaturized circuitry together to develop a watch called the Pulsar. It was totally electronic. It had no moving pieces at all.

Instead, the Pulsar, like the Accutron, used a quartz crystal and a small battery that caused the quartz to vibrate. But the Pulsar used these vibrations to transmit a high-frequency signal to electronic circuits in a miniature computer inside the watch. This circuitry counted the vibrations of the quartz and signaled digital numbers on the dial to change at the appropriate time. The dial did not have hands and numbers from one to twelve. Instead, it had a rectangular face covering a series of electronic parts called diodes, which emit light. When a button was pushed, the battery sent power to these diodes to show the correct time in digits.

This new electronic timekeeper, featuring computer circuitry and digital numbers, soon became popular in clock faces too. Dials never went completely

The Pulsar digital watch had no moving pieces and no hands on its dial. It showed the time with the help of light-emitting diodes.

out of style. They are still widely used in clocks and watches, and many people continue to prefer the traditional look of dials over digital readouts.

One drawback of the Pulsar and similar watches using light-emitting diodes (LEDs) was that the time was not displayed continually because it required a lot of power to do so. Within a few years, this problem was solved. The Waltham Watch Company in Massachusetts was one of the first to produce a watch using a liquid crystal display (LCD) instead of an LED. These LCD watches still used a small battery, a quartz crystal, and complicated circuitry, but they had a constant time display. This was possible because they used liquid crystals that reflected the light around them. The time display was brightest in sunlight but could also be seen in normally lighted rooms. The Japanese company Seiko added extra back lighting to many of its LCD watches so the time display could be seen more easily in dim or dark places.

Multifunction Watches

With the introduction of quartz crystals, wristwatches became as accurate as most people might ever need. Buyers began to take extreme accuracy for granted, so this feature was no longer enough to convince them to choose a particular product. Watchmakers began to explore different ways of attracting buyers.

During the 1970s and 1980s, watches offered many functions besides timekeeping. Watches that had calculators, calendars, stopwatches, alarms, message beepers, and other attractions were made by Seiko and other companies.

An American security company

called Communication Control Systems carried the development of multifunction wristwatches even further. They designed an inexpensive watch that doubled as a lie detector. Inside the watch was a tiny silicon chip with a voice analyzer. At the bottom of the watch was a row of eight tiny diodes. The voice analyzer measured stress and relayed it to the diodes. Supposedly, a person wearing the watch could tell if someone else was under stress, and therefore probably lying, if very few of the diodes were lit during a conversation.

Another unusual multifunction watch was developed by the Sharp Corporation in 1981. This watch had an alarm. When the preset time arrived, a voice, not a bell or buzzer, announced the time. For example, a pleasant voice might say, "It's 7:15 A.M." If the alarm was not turned off, the voice reminded the owner five minutes later by announcing, "It's 7:20. Please hurry." The voice told the time every five minutes until it was turned off.

Multifunction watches are often made for use in specific sports: Highly

Multifunction watches caught on in the 1970s and still interest consumers. The Seiko watch on the right features a personal pager.

waterproof scuba-diving watches can calculate diving depths. Those made for pilots can show altitude. Others are designed to meet the needs of skiers, racers, and sailboarders.

Although watches now fill many practical needs, they are still seen as objects of fashion and beauty. Today, people can buy watches in a huge variety of styles, ranging in price from

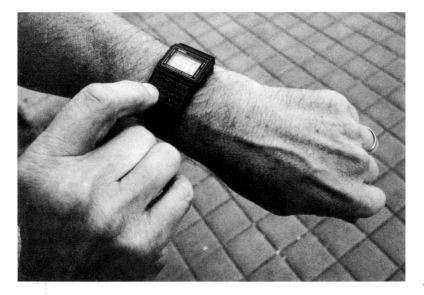

Today, watches fill many practical needs. This watch, for example, includes storage of telephone numbers, which can be displayed on the watch face.

Some watches offer more fanciful features, such as a dial decorated with the popular cartoon character, Mickey Mouse.

from the Swiss company Patek Philippe sold for $2.7 million. People choose watches as an expression of their personality or status. Some watches have dial faces that picture company logos, popular characters such as Mickey Mouse, or colorful scenes.

Another example of watches designed to appeal to different tastes is Le Clip. In 1986, a watch attached to a piece of plastic in the shape of a large clothespin was created. This watch was designed by Michael Jordi, the son of a Swiss watchmaker. Mechanically, the watch is similar to most others and is operated by a small battery and a quartz crystal. The dial and plastic clip are decorated in more than two hundred different designs. In one year, Jordi sold more than one million Le Clips in Europe before the watch was even available in the United States.

In many ways, Le Clip demonstrates how far watchmaking has come since the first Nuremberg egg was created. It is what Peter Henlein and his colleagues dreamed of 480 years ago: small, portable, lightweight, and accurate. Although the ordinary person is now satisfied with the accuracy and convenience of watches and clocks, the same cannot be said for scientists.

ninety-nine cents for a plastic disposable watch to fourteen thousand dollars or more for a diamond-encrusted Rolex. Some watches are now collectors' items, and many people pay hundreds or even thousands of dollars for handcrafted heirlooms. In 1989, for example, one handcrafted pocket watch

Expanding the Boundaries of Time and Space

For most people, a watch or clock that is accurate to within one minute a year is good enough. Scientists, however, use clocks that are thousands of times more accurate, and they are developing clocks that will be even more precise. These incredibly exact timepieces are called atomic clocks.

Atomic Clocks

Atomic clocks work on much the same principle as quartz clocks. But instead of being regulated by quartz, which vibrates exactly 100,000 times a second, atomic clocks use other elements. In these elements, the atoms—the tiny, constantly moving particles that are the building blocks of all matter—vibrate far more rapidly than the atoms of a quartz crystal.

The first atomic clock was developed in 1948 by a physicist named Louis Essen at the National Physical Laboratory in Middlesex, England. With his colleagues, Essen used complex measuring devices to keep track of the movement of atoms of cesium, which is a white, silvery metal. Other elements had been studied, but their atoms moved more slowly than those of cesium or they were less easy to work with. Essen's team determined that cesium atoms move exactly 9,192,631,770 times each second. They realized that this consistent and extremely rapid rate—nearly ninety-two thousand times faster than a

Many atomic clocks do not really look much like clocks. But they are among the most precise timekeeping pieces in the world.

quartz crystal—could be used to greatly improve the accuracy of timekeeping.

In atomic clocks, the main component is a long, vacuum-sealed tube made of an aluminum alloy. A beam of cesium atoms is sent through this tube. Carefully tuned radio waves beamed into the tube make the cesium atoms move. A device called a detector counts the movements of the atoms. When the atoms move at the known rate of cesium atoms, the detector sends a signal to a piece of quartz. Then, the quartz sends its own signal to an electric motor that moves the clock forward one second. The latest atomic clocks are accurate to ten-billionths of a second a day, or about four-millionths of a second a year.

Everyday Uses for Atomic Clocks

Atomic clocks can be used in many ways to provide people with information that would not be available otherwise. In advanced societies like that of the United States, these clocks are used to make everyday life a bit better. For instance, they help to more precisely regulate the flow of electricity. They are used to synchronize traffic lights in major cities, such as Los Angeles, to adjust computer hardware, and to track the center of earthquakes. Two of the most important uses for atomic clocks are in navigation and in setting a worldwide standard for correct time.

Modern navigational systems on the sea and in the air use radio signals to communicate the time in microseconds, or millionths of a second. But that precision is not good enough for space travel. The radio signals that are used to direct missions into outer space

Atomic clocks have many uses, including synchronizing traffic lights in major cities.

need to be timed to nanoseconds, or billionths of a second. Without such accurate timing, a spacecraft could go so far off its planned course that it could bypass or crash into the planet it was headed for. If this happened, enormous amounts of time, money, and information would be lost.

Atomic clocks also set the standard for timekeeping all over the world. Today, scientists and military forces worldwide set their clocks to reflect Coordinated Universal Time (UTC). The clocks of national governments, television networks, airlines, and other large organizations also get their time information from UTC, and the rest of us set our clocks and watches according to those sources. Now, the whole world tells time by one standard.

UTC is based on readings from a

Spacecraft of all types rely on the precise timekeeping ability of atomic clocks to stay on course.

network of fifty atomic clocks in various countries. Signals from all fifty clocks are sent to the Bureau International de l'Heure (BIH) in Paris, where they are adjusted using complex mathematical formulas. The BIH determines when "leap seconds" must be added to international time to compensate for minor fluctuations in the earth's rotation. The adjusted UTC is then relayed to clocks in all countries.

For instance, Chinese scientists in Beijing, Shanghai, and Xi'an tune in their television sets to a Soviet station every night at 9:59 P.M. By seeing how long it takes to receive the TV signal, they can test the accuracy of the atomic clocks that keep the time in China.

Scientific Uses for Atomic Clocks

Atomic clocks also enable scientists to study things that require extreme accuracy. For example, physicists and geolo-

gists use these clocks to make the precise measurements needed to calculate the age of the earth and the universe and to test an idea called the theory of special relativity.

Physicists can tell a lot about the age of matter by measuring how long it takes the atoms of a particular substance to decay. That rate of decay is known as the element's half-life. In the process of decay, the atoms of radioactive elements release nuclear particles and, in doing so, become atoms of the next lighter element on the periodic chart of the elements. For instance, atoms of uranium change into atoms of radium, and atoms of radium become atoms of radon. These changes keep taking place until the original atoms of uranium are transformed into atoms of lead, which are stable and do not continue to change.

The half-life of some elements is so short that physicists need to count picoseconds, or trillionths of a second. Some use even smaller measurements called femtoseconds, which are thousandths of a picosecond. Measuring these tiny parts of seconds was impossible before the invention of the atomic clock.

Atomic clocks are also important in the study of the special theory of relativity, which helps scientists understand more about the nature of time. This theory is based on a discovery made by the famous physicist Albert Einstein. In 1905, Einstein found that time does not always pass at the same rate but is affected by motion and gravity. Simply put, a rapidly moving clock ticks more slowly than a clock at rest. The faster the clock is moving, the more slowly time passes.

This theory was tested in 1971. Four cesium clocks were sent around the

Scientists use atomic clocks in their studies of Albert Einstein's special theory of relativity.

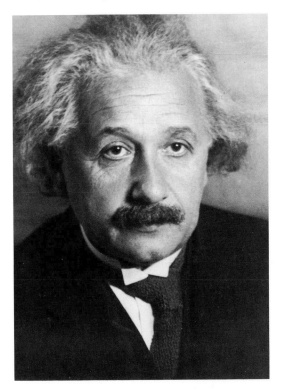

world on jet airplanes, first eastward and then westward. Since the earth spins eastward, the plane heading east traveled faster than the one heading west. Because of the speed of the planes and the gravitational forces exerted on them, the clock on the plane traveling east was expected to be 315 nanoseconds behind the one traveling west. The test results nearly matched the estimate, essentially verifying the theory. Only atomic clocks can measure time precisely enough to explore this theory further. This knowledge will affect clocks going into space because space vehicles move many thousands of miles per second.

Latest Atomic Clocks

Today, there are many types of atomic clocks, ranging in size from mantel clocks to grandfather clocks. But they are not designed with the beauty of their earlier counterparts. They are purely functional. Various models have been described as looking like filing cabinets or suitcases. Currently, the world's most accurate clock is in Brunswick, Germany. It can measure time within one second every 900,000 years.

Deep under the ground in Boulder, Colorado, sits the most accurate clock in the United States. This cesium clock, called NBS-6, is accurate to within one second in 300,000 years. Operated by the Time and Frequency Division of the National Institute of Standards and Technology (NIST), NBS-6 is used to determine the length of a second in this country. Despite its great precision, even this clock can make an error. It mistakenly thought that 1990 was a leap year. For several days after February 28, it measured the time accurately to the billionth of a second but gave the wrong date.

Since the first atomic clocks were created, scientists around the world have competed to build the most accurate one. The United States has been in a race with Germany, Japan, and Canada to build the most accurate clock on earth. The people at NIST say the United States is in the lead. A five-person team of scientists at Boulder, led by Robert Drullinger, has developed a clock called NIST-7. Unlike any atomic clock before, it uses lasers instead of radio waves to keep the cesium atoms moving. In general, lasers are far more precise than radio waves.

NIST-7, housed in a multilayered metal cylinder about ten feet long, is expected to be better than the clock in Brunswick and ten times more accurate than NBS-6, measuring time to within one second in three million years. This clock is expected to be ready for use in the early 1990s. Scientists already predict that by fine-tuning and improving on what they already know, atomic clocks in the year 2010 may be accurate to within one second in ten billion years.

Clocks in the Future

Atomic clocks regulated by fast-moving cesium atoms seem to be the standard today, but already a new type of clock for science is on the horizon. In 1989, the Nobel Prize in physics was awarded to three scientists for their efforts to develop even more accurate devices for measuring time. The scientists were Norman Ramsey of Harvard University,

Wolfgang Paul of the University of Bonn in Germany, and Hans Dehmelt of the University of Washington in Seattle. They are performing research on trapped-ion clocks. An ion is an electrically charged atom, and trapping them is extremely difficult. It will probably be at least another decade before clocks using trapped-ion technology will be ready for use, but it is estimated that they could be as much as 100,000 times more accurate than today's best clocks.

What will these clocks of the future be used for? Certainly, they will be used in every way possible to help humans manage everyday life in an increasingly complex and fast-paced world. And considerable research is still needed if scientists are to determine the age of the universe with any precision. In the field of nuclear physics, an increasing amount of research is being done on

Norman Ramsey is one of three scientists awarded the Nobel Prize in physics for efforts to develop more accurate devices for measuring time.

Sophisticated clocks may someday help scientists unravel the many mysteries of the universe, including black holes.

the tiny particles that make up atoms. These particles move so rapidly that they are measured in picoseconds and femtoseconds, and more accurate clocks would greatly help researchers do their work.

The challenge of breaking time into such minute parts grows, in some cases, from nothing more than scientific curiosity. But scientists also look to more precise clocks for new ways of understanding the concept of time, the laws of the universe, and its many mysteries. Perhaps the next generation of clocks will help scientists understand the strange wells of gravity in outer space known as black holes. Some scientists think that in these holes, time slows down or even ceases to exist as we know it. Clocks may also help scientists prove and explore the existence of tachyons, tiny particles thought to move faster than light.

More accurate timekeeping will allow not only for more study of the universe but for more intense study of the scientific laws and theories that govern it. Some intriguing aspects of the theory of special relativity, for example, have yet to be adequately tested. According to the theory, people who engage in space travel will come back to earth younger than people of the same age who stayed home. Just as clocks slow down when they are put in motion, so does the human heart. And over time, this decrease in heart rate slows aging. It will take more research and more precise time measurement to discover the full implications of this idea.

Human beings have come to depend on specialized clocks in the fields of medicine, computers, communications, transportation, physics, and space exploration, among others.

The speed with which clock technology has developed in this century reflects the sense of speed that clocks helped introduce to our culture. Today, so many activities are planned and measured with split-second timing—a news broadcast, a rock song, a television commercial, an airline flight, a delicate medical procedure, a telephone call. We have come to take these precise measurements of time for granted. Scientists and clock makers of tomorrow will undoubtedly find many more ways to tell us the time and give us ideas of how to spend it.

Glossary

atomic clock: A complex device that uses the regular vibrations of cesium atoms to tell time in the most reliable and accurate way yet developed.

automata: Mechanical figures that move around a small, household clock; they are similar to the large jacks on tower clocks.

balance spring: The small piece of coiled metal that helps the mainspring control the gears in a watch.

clepsydra: The Greek name for a clock operated by water power.

clockwork: The connecting train of gears and wheels that move the hands in a mechanical clock.

escapement: The mechanical device that controls the rate of the wheels in the clock.

flextime: Working hours that do not fit into an eight-hour day, five days a week.

foliot balance: A weighted T-shaped bar added to the escapement to improve its ability to control the rate of the gears in the clock.

Greenwich time: The prime basis of standard time throughout the world; also called Universal Time.

horology: The science of measuring time.

jack: An automated figure, usually a religious or military figure, that moves near the dial of tower clocks.

liquid crystal display (LCD): On a digital watch, a readout of digits or letters composed of segments of liquid crystal that reflect light.

mainspring: The small piece of coiled metal that controls the rate of the wheels in a watch.

marine chronometer: A spring-controlled timepiece that keeps accurate time at sea and helps sailors correctly determine their longitude.

pendulum: A rod with a ball at the end that swings back and forth. It controls the rate of the gears in a clock, as the escapement and foliot balance did in the earliest clocks.

quartz: A mineral that, when specially cut and processed, vibrates at a constant speed. Quartz crystals have been used to regulate the gears of clocks and watches.

slave clock: A clock without an internal source of power, such as an electric clock.

time clock: A mechanical device that marks the time an employee arrives at and leaves work.

For Further Reading

Jeanne Bendick, *The First Book of Time.* New York: Franklin Watts, 1963.

Timothy Levi Biel, *Atoms: Building Blocks of Matter.* San Diego: Lucent Books, 1990.

Walter Buehr, *Keeping Time.* New York: Putnam's, 1960.

Lesley Coleman, *A Book of Time.* New York: Thomas Nelson, 1971.

Ken Sobol, *The Clock Museum.* New York: McGraw-Hill, 1967.

Works Consulted

Isaac Asimov, *The Near East*. Boston: Houghton Mifflin, 1968.

Isaac Asimov, "The Two Masses," in *The World Treasury of Physics, Astronomy, and Mathematics*, edited by Timothy Ferris. Boston: Little, Brown, 1991.

Ralph M. Barnes, *Motion and Time Study*. New York: John Wiley & Sons, 1968.

John Boslough, "The Enigma of Time," *National Geographic*, March 1990.

Frederick James Britten, *Old Clocks and Watches and Their Makers*. New York: Bonanza Books, 1956.

Eric Bruton, *Clocks and Watches, 1400-1900*. New York: Frederick A. Praeger, 1967.

Carlo Cipolla, *Clocks and Culture, 1300-1700*. New York: Walker & Company, 1967.

John G. Clark, David M. Katzman, Richard D. McKinzie, and Theodore A. Wilson, *Three Generations in Twentieth Century America*. Homewood, IL: The Dorsey Press, 1977.

Harrison J. Cowan, *Time and Its Measurement*. Cleveland, OH: The World Publishing Company, 1958.

T.P. Camerer Cuss, *The Country Life Book of Watches*. Middlesex: Country Life Books, 1967.

Will Durant, *The Story of Civilization. Vol. 4, The Age of Faith*. New York: Simon & Schuster, 1950.

Encyclopedia Americana. Vol. 28. Danbury, CT: Grolier, 1985.

B.T. Fraser, *Time: The Familiar Stranger*. Amherst: The University of Massachusetts Press, 1987.

C.W. Hering, *The Lure of the Clock*. New York: Bonanza Books, 1932.

Peter Hood, *How Time Is Measured.* Oxford: Oxford University Press, 1969.

Derek Howse, *Greenwich Time and the Discovery of the Longitude.* Oxford: Oxford University Press, 1980.

Chester Johnson, *What Makes a Clock Tick?* Boston: Little, Brown, 1969.

David S. Landes, *Revolution in Time.* Cambridge, MA: Harvard University Press, 1983.

François Le Lionnais, *The Orion Book of Time.* New York: Orion Press, 1959.

D. Allan Lloyd, *Old Clocks.* London: Ernest Benn, 1972.

Samuel L. Macey, *Clocks and the Cosmos: Time in Western Life and Thought.* Hamden, CT: Archon Books, 1980.

Samuel L. Macey, *The Dynamics of Progress: Time, Method and Measure.* Athens: University of Georgia Press, 1989.

Elbert S. Maloney, *Dutton's Navigation and Piloting.* Annapolis, MD: Naval Institute Press, 1985.

James Remington McCarthy, *A Matter of Time.* New York: Harper Brothers, 1947.

McGraw-Hill Encyclopedia of Science and Technology, 6th ed. New York: McGraw-Hill, 1987.

Willis I. Milham, *Time & Timekeepers.* New York: Macmillan, 1944.

Harry E. Neal, *The Mystery of Time.* New York: Julian Messner, 1966.

Benjamin W. Niebel, *Motion and Time Study.* Homewood, IL: Richard D. Irwin, 1982.

Brooks Palmer, *The Book of American Clocks.* New York: Macmillan, 1928.

About the Author

■ ■

A. J. Brackin is a graduate of the Universal College in California. She has studied history, German, and Russian.

For several years, she has worked as a researcher and writer. She enjoys reading and writing biographies as well as many other subjects. Recently, she has also worked in school and day-care settings with children of various ages.

Over the years, she has traveled extensively through Europe, Canada, and most of the United States. She lives in Long Beach, California.

Picture Credits

■■■■■■■■■■■■■■■■■■■■■■■■■■■■■■■■■■■

Cover photo: © 1990, Comstock

AP/ Wide World Photos, 33 (top), 78 (both), 81

The Bettmann Archive, 12, 15, 20, 26 (top), 28, 36, 38, 39 (bottom), 48 (both), 54 (both), 61, 64, 66 (bottom), 70, 72 (bottom)

Bettmann/Hulton, 60

The Connecticut Historical Society, Hartford, Connecticut, 40

Kevin Hall, 14, 22, 30, 34, 41, 57, 62, 69

Harvard University, 84

Historical Pictures Service, 13, 16 (both), 18, 19, 21, 24, 25, 26 (bottom), 27, 29 (top), 31 (top), 32, 35, 49, 50 (bottom), 66 (top), 67 (top)

Library of Congress, 46, 50 (top), 51, 55, 56, 59, 63, 83

NASA, 82, 85

National Archives, 52

National Maritime Museum, 58 (right)

Courtesy of the Time Museum, Rockford, Illinois, 17, 29 (bottom), 31 (bottom), 37, 39 (top), 42, 43 (both), 44, 58 (left), 67 (bottom), 68, 71, 72 (top), 75, 77, 79, 80

Timex, 74

Victoria & Albert Museum, 65